# GRIEF
# AND
# GROWTH

# GRIEF
# AND
# GROWTH

---

## *A Manual for*
## *Educators and Counselors*

Wendy H. Davenson
LMFT, LADC, CT

**To order additional copies of this book, contact:**
Xlibris Corporation
1-888-795-4274
www.Xlibris.com
Orders@Xlibris.com
20818

# CONTENTS

This work is dedicated to my husband

M. Lee Davenson

and to my father

Norman W. Howard

"My love is a gift of feeling"

The 2003 Publication of this manual
is dedicated to my staunchest supporters:

Beaver, Jeff and Jenna, Betsey, Mom,
my cousins from Boston, Chicago,
and New Hampshire,

and to Tom

with gratitude for their never ending
encouragement,

faith, love, and support.

# ACKNOWLEDGMENTS

I want to acknowledge the contributions of Peter Lynch, MSW and Bess Bailey Chosak, MSN for their invaluable teaching, contributions, and caring. Peter, Joanna Martin and I talked of writing a book on loss many years ago. The discussions have remained with me and were catalysts for me to write this manual.

# A PARABLE

Once upon a time, twin boys were conceived in the same womb. Seconds, minutes, hours passed as two dormant lives developed. The spark of life glowed until it fanned fire with the formation of their embryonic brains. With their brains came feelings and with feeling, perception; a perception of surrounding, of each other, of self.

When they perceived the life of each other and their own life, they knew that life was good, and they laughed and rejoiced, the one saying, "Lucky are we to have this world," and the other chiming, "Blessed be the Mother's blood." So they sang, "How great is the love of the Mother that gave us this life and each other."

Each budded and grew arms and fingers, lean legs and stubby toes. They stretched their lungs, churned and turned in their newfound world. They explored their world and in it found the life cord that gave them life from the precious Mother's blood. So they sang, "How great is the love of the Mother, that she shares all she has with us." And they were pleased and satisfied with their lot.

Weeks passed into months, and with the advent of each new month they noticed a change in each other, and each began to see a change in himself. "We are changing," said the one. "What can it mean?" "It means," replied the other, "that we are drawing near to birth." An unsettling chill crept over the two, and they both feared for they knew that birth meant leaving all their world behind.

Said one, "Were it up to me, I would live here forever." "We must be born," said the other. "It has happened to all others who were here." For indeed there was evidence of life there before, as the Mother had borne others. "But might there be no life after birth?" cried the one. "Do we not shed our life cord and also the blood tissues? And have you ever talked to one who has been born?? Has anyone ever re-entered the womb after birth? No!" He fell into despair, and in his despair he moaned, "If the purpose of conception and all of our growth is that it be ended in birth, then truly our life is absurd!"

Resigned to despair, the one stabbed the darkness with his unseeing eyes as he clutched his precious life cord to his chest and said, "If this is so, and life is absurd, then there really can be no Mother." "But there is a mother," protested the other. "Who else gave us nourishment and our world?"

Thus, while one raved and despaired, the other resigned himself to birth and placed his trust in the hands of the Mother. Hours ached into days, and days fell into weeks, And it came time. Both knew their birth was at hand, and both feared what they did not know. As the one was first to be conceived, so he was the first to be born, the other following after. They cried as they were born into the light. And coughed out and gasped the dry air. And when they were sure they had been born, they opened their eyes seeing for the first time, and they found themselves cradled in the warm love of the Mother. They lay open-mouthed and awe struck before the beauty and truth they could not have hoped to know.

—*Author unknown*

# PREFACE

This manual continues to be written and revised out of need: my need to disseminate accurate information on what is often thought of as an "unspeakable" subject, and an increasing number of individuals, counselors, and school personnel requesting the material in this manual. Therapeutically this manual allows me to recognize my urgency for continuing bonds with the significant people who have died and are no longer actively in my life. It also enables me to teach the concepts of loss and grief within larger contexts other than death.

This book is about helping children and adults who have experienced loss and are grieving. It is about understanding grief as a deep sadness, an intense suffering experienced as a result of being deprived or bereft of someone or something that is highly valued, and as a vast sorrow. It is about understanding that loss is a person's view or perception of what is a loss and not some external reality that determines grief. It is about grieving as an active process that can take many paths and directions.

The loss process is complex and is experienced in numerous facets of life. Children of addictions experience loss, children who are sexually, physically, or emotionally violated experience loss, children whose families relocate to different geographic regions experience loss, and children who are bullied in school experience loss. Clearly children experience loss in many varied ways. Adults experience loss in the above mentioned ways too. They experience loss developmentally for themselves and for their children, as well as physically, spiritually, emotionally, and financially.

The experience of loss impacts accessibility to learning and healthy life development. This manuscript allows me to teach other helping professionals to comprehend the depth and pervasiveness of the loss and grieving process for children, youth, and families. My hope is that through this manual, helping professionals will assist their clients, students, and families with this very difficult and painful state known as grief.

This grief process about which I write continues to be a growth and learning experience for me, even years after the deaths of my husband and my father. While their losses have been truly significant, I have had the benefits of watching and learning from my children as they have grown, matured, and learned from the losses that so impacted their lives.

Family processes are wonderful to observe and I am grateful that I have been able to watch my own. I am inordinately proud of my family. We have been a wonderful support system for one another.

A very special thanks to Peter Gow III, for his editing and unselfish gifts of time and support, to my brother, Stephen and sister-in-law, Dimiti for rescuing me from my computer panic, and to Tom for his quiet strength, patience and support.

Wendy H. Davenson

# CHAPTER 1

## THE IMPORTANCE
## OF UNDERSTANDING
## LOSS AND GRIEF

There are few psychological conditions that are as unrecognized and as debilitating to growth and achievement in school and healthy life development as is the experience of grief, i.e., *the deep sadness and poignant distress one can feel in response to a perceived loss.* Restated, when we have this feeling, it is the result of believing that we have been reft; that is, we think we have been severely deprived or robbed of someone or something. The resulting feeling of such deep sadness can cause other impairing emotions and thoughts and consequently dull our capacities. When we experience profound grief, we have difficulty focusing on other matters. We feel lonely. We feel alienated. We feel as if our lives are totally out of control and in chaos. We feel different and frightened. We feel pain.

When we are grieving, we are at a mental disadvantage in that our ability to focus and concentrate are impaired. This is not a condition of altered pathology in the psycho-neurotic sense, although grieving people fear the feelings they experience could signify some form of mental illness. Grief as a noun should be distinguished as a normal behavior, different from a neurotic or psychotic depression, even though depression also is characterized by intense sadness. The conditions producing grief are not the same as for clinical depression as grief is a situational depression, resulting from a severe loss. Thus, to experience grief is not in and of itself evidence of a mental illness. In truth, if one does not feel grief after the loss of a loved one, we would have cause for concern.

As a verb, *grieving* is a more encompassing term than *grief*. It includes the feelings and behaviors that accompany grief. The grieving process can include feelings of anxiety, hopelessness, physical pain, and fear, some of which may seem reasonable while others may appear highly irrational. As a verb, grieving is a process that takes various paths with various outcomes. These outcomes can lead to reinvesting in a new life, one in which the felt loss is missing, or to remaining in a debilitative state. The chronic experience of grief can precipitate in some people clinical depression and the need for pharmaceutical intervention. Thus, it is extremely important that when our clients or students are suffering deep sadness from a felt loss that we help them. It is not our job as counselors or school personnel to judge the grieving process of our constituents. It is our task to be aware and to respond appropriately to them. And honestly, nearly every one of our clients or students will, at some time, experience some level of grief.

In other words, nearly everyone has grieved or will grieve because of the loss of someone they value, hold in high esteem, and love. This is something we all understand. We grieve when we lose or are denied what we highly value. Even the loss of valued opportunities can cause us great sadness. When we lose something of less value, we experience less sadness. Thus it is not only the loss that precipitates grief. Rather it is the magnitude of the value placed on what is lost or denied that determines the magnitude of the grief response. It is the closeness or value of the relationship or the magnitude of the investment of the self in what is lost that determines the intensity of the grief response. Thus feeling robbed or deprived of valued opportunities or recognition, or even the fear of losing a valued event in the future can cause intense sadness and grief.

What then does profound sadness cause? First, we know that grief is associated with the impairment of certain cognitive and emotional abilities. It does not matter what the reasons are for our sadness—good, bad, rational, irrational—when we grieve, we are at a marked cognitive and emotional disadvantage. When clients or students are intensely sad, they too find it difficult to carry out many of their desired obligations or our expectations for them. And even if their sadness does not seriously impair them, there is likely to be some negative impact on their achievements, emotions, and behavior. Therefore the grief of our clients and students should be of concern.

Second, profound grief also precipitates other dysfunctional feelings, such as resentment, anger, estrangement from relationships and feelings of loneliness. To be sure, these disabling emotions can occur without experiencing the pain of grief. Nonetheless, negative feelings of painful sadness are likely to precipitate these emotions and other problems. Therefore when people suffer sadness they are at further disadvantage because of the added emotional issues they experience. And when they suffer from such emotions as anger, they may not recognize their anger as partially attributable to their grief. Thereby it may be difficult for them to deal with either their anger or their sadness.

To further compound the problems of grievers, their peers and some adults may react to them with pity or disdain and not compassion—especially if their grieving is chronic and public. Grieving people may be expected to "just get over it." If grievers do not make their pain public, however, others may believe and behave toward them as "uncaring." Many more unfortunate kinds of responses toward grievers can be described. If important people in the lives of grieving people express judgement, pity, disdain, fear, or criticism, the grievers are not being helped. If significant people show their misunderstanding of grief feelings with platitudes, euphemisms, or ingratiating comments, the grieving individuals will distance themselves from the very people who should be support systems at a time when they need them the most. On the other hand, if grievers are responded to in ways that help them to express and manage their grief, there can be beneficial effects. Of course, for people to manage their grief well will depend upon their emotional health as well as the responses of others and other variables. This is where you come in. You can be an important feature in the "other variables" category.

Since the emotional adjustment, backgrounds, and social circumstances of grieving people vary, their grief responses will also vary. This of course, is true for adults as well. Among some grievers, their grief may be chronic and intense for longer periods of time than for others. Some people in grief will express their grief publicly while others will do so privately. Others may repress their grief, in which case their grief will still function while they continue to deny it. For the helping professional, grievers who repress their grief are more difficult to counsel. If grief is repressed, other symptoms of pathology can present, such as sublimation, projection, depression, acting out behavior, and these reactions may further jeopardize their mental health.

In summary, while the magnitude, duration, patterns, and effects of grief vary, there is no escape for any of us from the distress of feeling deprived of someone or something we love or highly value. We can, however, seek to foster in ourselves and in our constituents the more positive outcomes that occur when grief is appropriately managed. If we do, we will contribute to positive mental health growth in our clients and students.

Our challenge is not to expect our clients or students to avoid grief, because they cannot. Rather, we need to teach them how to reduce the debilitating effects of their grief. If we can, they will reap the benefits and growth that grieving well can provide. They will appreciate their lives with their lost loved ones of yesterday and maintain healthy bonds with them long into the future, all without complicating new relationships and opportunities. Restated, responding to grieving individuals in certain ways is a necessary prelude to not only their psychological adjustment to their loss but to reducing the negative impact that grief can have on their futures. Loss, when well managed, is personal growth.

So now, let us look further into the types of losses and intense suffering that individuals experience. These types of loss include perceptions of having lost someone or something that was highly valued, the *fear* or anticipation of losing something highly valued, and the felt loss of something which one never had but to which one felt entitled.

The loss of a parent, precious pet, or important relationship are examples of losses that can have devastating impacts on children, youth, and adults. When, for example, a child loses a parent to death, and that student has been dependent on that parent for comfort, security, self-identity, and motivation to achieve certain goals, the possible response can range on a continuum from psychiatric illness to healthy adaptation. The death of a pet can be a very painful loss for children and adults. Pets become members of the family in that they are constant companions and often aids. Assistance and guide dogs as well as K-9 dogs are not only "best friends" with their handlers but essential aids. Recognition of the impact of a beloved pet's death is essential. Relationships for children exceed family relationships. Peer relationships, athletic team relationships, dating relationships are only a few examples. Students get very involved emotionally in these associations. The loss of a relationship for youth and adults can be devastating and tragic. How people adapt to these losses is vital. In the case of healthy adaptation to grief, the person experiences the pain of the loss, but understands and accepts the pain while learning to reinvest the needed emotional energy into life without the loved one.

Feared or anticipatory loss can be as obvious as a person who is living with a terminally ill relative or as unrecognized as an adolescent/adult who remains in an abusive relationship for fear of losing the status of being involved in a relationship. Feared loss includes the anxiety that often accompanies the anticipation of being separated from someone, as in the case of a high school student leaving home for the first time. Some students fear leaving the security of high school to embark on the unknown and actually unconsciously sabotage their senior year success. Fear of failure in test taking is another example of anticipatory loss.

The loss of something which one never had but to which one feels entitled could be an award or a recognition that goes to another student or school. Losing an "expected" athletic title, award, or recognition are examples of this type of loss. Students who feel they were supposed to be selected as the winner of the school election and do not get the award, grieve the loss of that expectation. Another example of this type of loss is the student who thought she did well on a test and actually failed it. As parents, educators, and counselors, we cannot underestimate the impact of these losses on students, socially, emotionally and academically.

Thus, the loss of a parent, the fear of losing a loved one or a precious pet, and the loss of a highly desired reward or some valued entitlement are three conditions that can produce intense suffering in our students. So what does this mean for us as educators and counselors? It means that it is our task to assist clients and students who are grieving to understand the nature and sources of their grief and how best to manage their grief in the context of meeting their other needs.

Unless people can learn to make sense of their strongly felt losses, they are at a marked disadvantage as human beings and more particularly, as students accessible to learning. As educators and counselors, our professional tasks are also impaired. Unless we, ourselves, fully understand the loss process and the tasks inherent within that process, it will be difficult for us to help children effectively. It is our job, as teachers, mentors, coaches, counselors, and motivators to teach youth to make sense of what they have lost or what they fear they will lose and to help them to deal with their grief in the healthiest manner possible. It is our job to be available to grieving families and help them learn to grieve openly and in health.

If that is our aim, we must understand our own loss and grief experiences first and foremost. Unfortunately as parents, educators and counselors, we can and sometimes do, make matters worse. There is a truism about life: How we respond to others determines whether we help or harm them. Our own unresolved loss issues can have ramifications on how we respond to the loss issues of our constituents!

We must therefore help youth and those who work with them understand the pain of loss, accept the loss as something that cannot be reversed and deal, in an appropriate manner, with realistic and unrealistic fears that might accompany the loss. In doing so, we can offer the hope that people suffering loss can and do find new lives. They can and will withdraw the energy from the grieving action and invest it in life as it is without what was lost. They can and will learn to live full and happy lives.

We can also help grievers accept and adapt to new roles that may be thrust on them, as a result of their losses. There may be temporary conditions such as a parent being hospitalized or deployed overseas, or permanent situations of parental death that require new roles and responsibilities from a child, adolescent, or adult. Some of these new roles may be perceived while others may be actual. For example, many well-meaning adults tell a child that he must now be the man of the house in his father's absence. This places stress on a child as he does not possess the skills needed to fulfill such a role. Our helping role may be to assist the youth to adapt to conditions by creating new and beneficial life skills.

It is important to take into account the more subtle forms of loss that can cause grief. A change in one's roles, security, or daily routine can produce a sense of loss with resultant suffering. The grief that might be associated with a lost school election or other intensely desired position may require a different form of compassionate response than a child who loses a parent to deployment or death. There are losses that result in grief that are quite reasonably expected such as in the death of an aged grandparent. Do not be misled into thinking that because the grandparent was aged that the pain of the loss should be less intense. In all of these examples, it is the relationship between what is lost and the child that determines the intensity of the loss reaction. For these reasons, helping professionals need to look closely at the nature of the perceived loss and resulting grief that a student is experiencing in order to determine the appropriate response.

There is another typical perceived loss that should be considered. Children can, at times, subconsciously experience a loss with grief at the same time that they psychologically deny that loss. Some gifted children have difficulty with peer relationships and while they feel the loss and grieve it, they typically deny it and engross themselves in an academic pursuit. When grief is the result of a loss that is denied, it is extremely difficult to address the loss.

Helping professionals will not, however, sufficiently understand perceived loss unless they also are aware of the intensity with which that loss is experienced. They need to know about the source of such felt loss. In this regard, one may experience a loss that is based on reality. On the other hand, one can be unrealistic or misinformed. A student, for example, may unrealistically believe that he or she is prepared to take a test and not do well, or feel deserving of an honor for which he or she has not met the criterion, or misjudge the consequences of what will happen when a parent is sent off to war or when a divorce occurs. Perceptions of loss vary in their type and in their relevance. There may be greater risk because of the psychological and physical states brought to a loss situation. Youth who are already experiencing depression are obviously more at risk when faced with other perceived losses than those students who are more psychologically healthy.

Intensive suffering, of course, can be the result of simultaneously experiencing one or all of these types of loss. For example, a child may intensely suffer from having lost a parent through death, while at the same time feel that this loss was unfair and that he or she did not deserve to be without a father. It is worthwhile to examine the causes of each type of perceived loss because they differ in how they are acquired and in the response we should provide.

# CHAPTER 2

## THE EXPERIENCE OF
## LOSS AND GRIEF

Loss *is* a part of life. Permanently losing, or anticipating the loss of, a highly valued loved one, a person, a pet, or an object, while emotionally difficult and painful, can be a valuable experience from which we can grow and mature if we address it in a healthy way. It is, however, difficult to grasp the value of growth when the loss seems so catastrophic. Loss can be seen as so tragic that it is unspeakable, to which we respond with both horror and denial. Through our fear and discomfort with death or the loss of someone or something we value, we teach people how to fear not only loss and death but also how to fear change and growth. Without experiencing loss, however, we cannot experience certain types of growth.

As stated, there are few psychological conditions that are as unrecognized and as debilitating to growth and achievement in school and healthy life development as is grief. Remember that these types of loss include *perceptions* of having lost something that was highly valued, the *fear* or anticipation of losing something highly valued, and the *felt loss* of something which one never had but to which one felt entitled.

There are two types of primary losses, **developmental life cycle losses** and **emotionally challenging losses,** both of which can be unwelcome and challenging. There are normal developmental life stage losses such as leaving home to get married or the death of a twenty two year old cat. Emotionally challenging losses are the result of what are perceived as tragedies e.g. breaking up with boyfriend or truly emotionally challenging losses of death, loss of limb, living with abuse and violence, military deployment, and other situations. Both types of loss can be typical life experiences and both types can be experienced with fear and denial. When a loss occurs outside of the normal developmental life cycle, such as the death of a spouse at age 32, the cognitive and emotional states of grief can be exacerbated. If one considers life as a series of attachments and separations, grief is a common response. How individuals react to being separated from their attachments is the criterion of healthy adjustment.

In other words, developmental losses are normal expected losses that are to occur at somewhat prescribed times during the life cycle. When death or major loss occurs out of the sequence of the developmental life cycle, the loss reactions increase from emotionally challenging to tragic. The addition of a tragic component to the loss can make the resolution more challenging and more difficult to comprehend.

Accompanying both tragic and normal losses are "secondary losses". Secondary losses can be defined as painful reminders of the primary losses. These may be changes in one's status, identity, security, or routine that are associated with the loss. Secondary losses are often unrecognized and difficult to identify or understand by persons who are not grieving. Youth who have lost a parent, for example, are faced with many changes in their family organization that may not be obvious to others. Changes in financial security, family identity, routine, chores, and responsibility are just a few of these secondary losses. Secondary losses are daily challenges and constant painful reminders of the primary loss event.

# DEVELOPMENTAL LIFE CYCLE LOSSES

Our birth is our first experience with a developmental loss. We are thrust out of the warm, moist, protected world of the womb into the dry, cool air of disconnectedness. Perhaps this loss explains the newborn infant's confusion, rage, pain, fear, and anguish. Yet without that loss of the womb, the child's life cannot go on.

As we grow, we experience further developmental losses. We give up the breast or the bottle to master self-feeding. We progress from crawling to walking, from crib to big bed, from the security of being at home all day to expanding our environment by going to school and leaving the security of home and a parent behind. The transition to puberty is a developmental gain . . . and loss. As we grow older and our bodies change, we continue to experience developmental loss. For parents, having children is a developmental loss experience. The developmental task of adolescence is to leave home with a minimum amount of emotional baggage from unresolved family conflicts. That means that parents must learn to let go of their children, to allow them to have strong roots of values and love but wings with which to fly off on their own. Thus parenting is about letting go and with that, it brings critical but normal losses and gains for them and for their children.

Several years ago I found a poem that I will include here. This poem reflects the developmental growth process of letting go of our children so as to allow them to be the beautiful individuals they are. I read this poem at my daughter's wedding as it seemed a fitting poetic symbol of my letting go of this beautiful creature who became a beautiful, competent, wonderful adult. This poem came to me with an author unknown and therefore I cannot give credit to any author other than "unknown".

> *I see children as kites; you spend a lifetime trying to get them off the ground.*
> *You run with them until you're both breathless . . . they crash . . . they hit the rooftop . . .*
> *You patch and comfort, adjust and teach. You watch them lifted by the wind and assume that someday they will fly.*

*Finally, they are airborne; they need more string and you keep letting it out.*

*But with each twist of the twine there is a sadness that goes with the joy. The kite becomes more distant, and you know that it won't be long before the beautiful creature will cut the lifeline that binds you together and will soar as it is meant to soar, free and alone.*

*Only then do you know that you did your job.*

Author Unknown

We all have had vast experiences with change and loss, yet we underestimate the impact of developmental life cycle losses on ourselves and others. We minimize how well we all, even in preschool years, have learned to cope with these losses. Yet in truth, we each enter kindergarten as an expert in loss and change.

Another way of understanding the cycle of loss and gain is to rephrase it as change, transition, and growth. Change can be seen as external and situational. Transition can be the psychological process of adjusting to the change. An example of this process might be when you buy a new house. When you first move into a new home, it is strange and unfamiliar. Creaks and groans may seem frightening until such time as you actually adjust and feel comfortable with the noises. This process is the psychological adjustment to an external change. When this process is complete, growth occurs. Life is definitely about change, transition, and adaptation to change.

However it is viewed, we will continue this cycle of loss and gain throughout our lifetime. Most of our developmental losses are normal and predictable. They help prime and prepare us for the less common and emotionally more challenging losses that result from death, declining health, or divorce. In other words, life is a series of attachments and separations that are natural and common to everyone. How profound! Mental health is how we adjust to these attachments and separations. Life can be seen as 10% what happens to us and 90% how we react to these events.

# TRAGIC LOSSES

Death is an unwelcome loss and one of the most severe, although others can be just as unacceptable, including loss of health, loss of body parts, loss through divorce, loss of income, loss of pets, loss of a parent or spouse being called away to military duty, loss of someone in the hospital, or prison, loss through rape, loss of life savings, loss due to severe environmental conditions, even retirement. Each of these jarring, cataclysmic events stirs intense feelings, a deep sadness, and behaviors that we call "grief."

To put these unwelcome losses in the context of loss as a life experience is to emphasize one of the central truths about loss, grief, and bereavement. Inherent in the sadness of loss is the incredible potential for emotional gain and a renewed contract with life itself. So, even though loss is perceived as an unwelcome word, it presents us with the opportunity for growth, for new or renewed strength, new opportunities, insights, even wisdom.

There is an infinite number of ways that tragically induced losses can occur. There are losses connected with catastrophic environmental disasters, like earthquakes, fires, tornadoes, and hurricanes. There are losses resulting from wars, losses of limbs, sight, hearing and mental health. There is the loss of security associated with terrorism, as evidenced by the disaster of September 11, 2001.

Rape and other forms of abuse leave the victims with numerous loss issues to confront. These might include loss of virginity, power, control, self-esteem, youth, security, and assumptions of safety. The divorce process can be another severe emotional loss for parents and children. Many never fully recover from the trauma of the marital and family dissolution, disillusion, and disharmony.

Living in a home where there is active addiction presents emotional challenges for family members. The unpredictability of addictive behavior results in a chaotic environment for children and adults. The capricious behaviors of addiction can destroy a stable, predictable home environment where children can grow up with feelings of security, and safety. Thus, whether the experience of loss is developmental due to a change such as children being launched or due to losses of disease, disability, disaster, death, or divorce, the *process* of grieving is the same.

There is also the experience of loss of rewards to which individuals believe they are entitled. These rewards may include the love of another, grades in school, acceptance in a group, an expected gain or recognition. Again the grief experience follows the same path.

Grief is an experience of acute deprivation. Grief work can also be an emancipation from the bondage of the deceased. It is adjustment to an environment in which the deceased is missing. The experience is difficult, confusing, and exhausting. Contrary to popular opinion, one does not "get over" the death of a loved one, nor does one *want* to get over it. Grievers do want to feel better, to get over the pain of the loss, and to become more invested in the present, as it is without the deceased person.

## SECONDARY LOSSES

Secondary losses occur as a result or consequence of the initial loss and initiate their own grief and mourning reactions. Each secondary loss must be recognized and each one mourned. A secondary loss can be physical as in a relocation or it can be psychological and emotional as in the loss of a confidant or lover. These losses are intensely painful and often constant. According to noted author, Therese Rando (1986), an individual can sustain a psycho-social loss without an accompanying physical loss but every physical loss will produce psycho-social loss.

Secondary losses are often overlooked or misunderstood by friends, family, and school or other professional personnel. They are deeper, more personal changes that occur as a consequence of the primary loss and often are less readily identified. Such losses have incredible power and significance for the bereaved as they take the grieving process to a more intensely painful level. These may involve the loss of a valued role or identity, the loss of valued companionship, the loss of a hoped for future, the loss of security and the feeling of control, the loss of trust, the loss of a daily routine, and of course, the loss of concentration. The following are examples and explanations of other secondary losses.

**The loss of a role and the label that describes that role**

A parent whose child has died does not know how to respond to the question of "How many children do you have?" A female spouse is no longer labeled "Mrs." once her husband has died. A child does not know how to describe his "family" when to him, it is no longer a family when one parent lives in a different house.

**The loss of time, a childhood, or innocence**

There is a loss of time, perhaps a childhood, as a child must take on new roles and responsibilities resulting from a primary loss such as the death of a parent. This loss can further be applied to the loss of virginity or innocence when a young girl is raped. Children living in families with active addictions often lose their childhood as new adult roles are thrust on them in order to compensate for the non-functioning actively using addict parent. In the absence of a parent, new chores and responsibilities can be assigned that disallow what was formerly childhood or play time.

**The loss of interaction, companionship, confidant**

For children and youth, when a significant person leaves their life, they often grieve the loss of the friendship, the fun, the sharing of stories and secrets. "Who can I talk to now?" is a commonly asked question. When a parent dies, there are losses of companionship, adult interaction, and adult confidences. The surviving parent may lean on their children to fulfill these roles. High school students often feel their surviving parent leans on them too much.

When a best friend moves to a new geographic location, there can be a loss of all that accompanies being "best friends" with someone. Questions of "Where do I fit now?" or "Who will I eat lunch with now?" are common examples of the secondary losses surfacing.

### The loss of a future

Females whose fathers have died ask "Who will walk me down the aisle when I get married?" Adolescents often wonder if they will have to care for the surviving parent. Well—meaning adults often charge teenage sons with now being "the man of the house" upon the loss of their fathers. This is tremendous pressure on a young male and should not be placed on him! As evidenced by the World Trade Center disaster, some surviving widows committed suicide as they felt they were unable to live with a future without their husbands. This leaves more children to face a future life without either parent. Loss of limbs or use of the body leave questions about future directions for the afflicted person.

### The loss of identity

Now, who am I? Now, where do I fit? Now, what is our "family?" Adolescence is a time of identity formation. When death or divorce loss occur during this pivotal developmental time, a young person's sense of self can be truly assaulted by new demands, new roles and a sense of uncertainty. When living in a family with the secrecy of addictions, identity formation for youth is very unclear and difficult. Identity formation for a child who has been sexually molested is savagely altered. Even when an adult loses a parent, there is a loss of identity. Many adults feel like an orphan when their last surviving parent dies. In divorce, many women return to their maiden names in order to seek a new sense of identity.

Families living with active addictions may never have

developed individual or family identities. Thus the task of identity formation is thrust upon them long after it should have been completed. And many of these families have no idea how to create an identity.

### The loss of security and control

It is not uncommon to hear "If he dies, will I? Will you? Who will die next?" Death undermines feelings of security and control! We probably never had any "control" over our life, but death is the ultimate reminder of all that we *cannot* control. Young children who lose parents often live with a vast loss of security and may compensate by trying to over-control their own lives. Referring to the September 11, 2001 World Trade Center/ Pentagon/Pittsburgh tragedy, several children lost both parents in the attacks. These children had their world totally altered in brief seconds. They naturally lost all feelings of security and control in "their child worlds". These events will impact their lives in ways that many people will be unaware, most significantly in the areas of security and control.

Another area of security and control lost may be that of financial security. This may impact children as it may necessitate physical changes in homes, schools, lifestyles, and certainly home climate. These physical changes lead to social and emotional changes. The domino effect of loss is clearly illustrated in secondary losses.

There is also a tremendous loss of security and control with sexual or physical violations.

### The loss of trust and confidence

These are the resulting feelings when security and control are lost. Children and youth have certain world-view assumptions of being safe and having things happen in the order in which they should occur. Tragedies such as the World Trade Center disaster shatter our trust and confidence in our life as we think we know it. It takes years of painful work for children to rebuild trust in life. As counselors and educators we focus on consistency as a necessary ingredient for healthy growth in children; yet when catastrophic events occur, they shatter that consistency of life. For children, their feelings of trust and confidence in the outside world and within themselves are also crushed.

### The loss of routine

When a parent dies or leaves the home, the routine of life at home is totally altered. Chores and responsibilities are reassigned but more significant is the emotional alteration of life without that significant person. This is loss of routine that occurs when a child lives with an actively using addict parent or a parent with mental illness. When the parent is sober and functioning, he or she can fulfill the parenting role but when under the influence of a substance or mental illness, the roles and responsibilities of the family often fall on the shoulders of the children. This is even more difficult for the children as the "when" this might occur is so unpredictable.

A secondary loss of routine is keenly felt when a person retires, is laid off, or fired from his/her professional career. What do you do when everyone else is going to work on Monday morning?

### The loss of concentration

Concentration or focus are often difficult as if there is an ongoing unconscious video of the loss event over which the survivor has no control. Forgetfulness, preoccupation, wandering, searching and wondering "What am I doing standing here?" are common blocks to concentration. I recommend carrying a note pad and using it to remind yourself of why you went wherever and for what. Another commonly heard comment is: "Wherever I am is not where I want to be". This is because the griever is still searching for the lost person/event and thus moves from place to place hoping to find what is missing. Driving is not recommended when in this confused state!

Secondary losses are faced by survivors on a daily basis. And they make the primary loss even more painful by keeping the pain constant. "Why am *I* in this situation?" "Will this ever end?" Grievers can feel overwhelmed by the secondary losses and in order to function, they often go into a survival mode. They function robotically and while they seem to survive the loss, the agony of the secondary losses makes the griever feel as if the grief will never subside. Secondary losses surface most intensely during the second year following the loss. The first year is often described as a year of numbness, while the second year following the loss can be more painful to the griever as the numbness has dissipated.

It is easy to make the point that a loss of a valued person, object, or event on which one feels dependent will produce some level of sadness in otherwise healthy individuals, while in others, the outcome may be depression. What is not so clear to most people is that when one loses or is denied anything or anyone of great value, a new challenge is forced—that of how the grieving person is to relate to a world without what has been lost or denied. This challenge can seem monumental and very painful. It requires a new world view and a new identity with one's world view.

Young people are in search of identity. Their critical world is relatively small, consisting mainly of family, peers, and school. Any loss that threatens their relationships in these settings is likely to produce grief and/or other debilitating reactions.

To be of assistance with students who experience the loss of identity through catastrophic loss and grief situations, one must take into account what the child has lost from the child's perspective. In adult vernacular, that loss is a void or denial of a relationship in the child's world, that they crave and yearn to have back. They feel they have lost who they are and want to be, relative to the loss of the relationship. They often suffer discomfort, exhibit restrictions on their motivation and feel a sense of insecurity. One need not suffer the death of a person to feel such a threat to one's sense of self. To be excluded from a team or friends may be to be shut out from a highly valued relationship, that in turn, could be the basis of a valued self-identity. Feeling excluded can produce intense sadness, especially for children and adolescents.

The questions then seem to be: What can we do to help children and youth who have suffered losses? When a person's identity is being challenged, how can we help? What should we not do so as to avoid making matters worse for the student or client?

Teachers, counselors, and friends must learn about loss as a growth process. They must recognize that secondary losses accompany the grief process and they must allow the grievers expression of their sorrow. We need to recognize that these are losses that a griever can feel on a *daily* basis and that make the griever feel as if "this painful process will never end." Our job is to assist in their adjustment to the reality of the loss and to the many assaults to their identity and self worth.

You cannot grieve for them! But you can be aware of both their primary and secondary losses, listen quietly, and offer reassurance. As stated earlier, these secondary losses are most felt during the second or third year after the primary loss. The first year of grief is learning to cope with holidays and special events, with numbness. The second year tends to be one of feeling the secondary losses, painfully, as the numbness wears off. One might say, "You try to pretend you are who you were but suddenly you know you are not who you were. So who are you?"

# CHAPTER 3

## THE PROCESS OF GRIEVING

The resolution of grief is a **process** with an unavoidable sequence of tasks and goals. It is a process in that there are a series of operations or steps, rather than a one-time episode or event. It is a journey with several outcomes, goals, and stages. Within each stage there are accompanying tasks for the griever to complete. This process of task accomplishment is *not* a lock-step process. One moves back and forth among the stages, sometimes at intervals of days or hours. There is no "one way to go," no "correct" way to grieve. Each individual grieves in his own way and on his own time frame—and this is acceptable.

Grieving is a process, often compared with the changing seasons. The *loss* itself can be likened to an enormous autumn electrical storm, charged and frightening, coinciding with the fall season when everything begins to change. This is similar to the start of the loss experience. The bleakness of the winter season is a comparison of the grief feeling of despair, when all feels cold, stark, and sad. The season of spring brings new growth and new beginnings. This phase correlates to the beginning of the griever reorganizing life around that which is lost. Summer corresponds to the time frame of reinvestment in the grief process. It is a time of withdrawing the emotional energy from the other seasons and seeing the fruits of one's labors, such as flowers, sunshine, and joy.

Grieving is difficult yet it can be a positive and healing growth process. Grieving is winding, jolting, ragged, and unpredictable.

It is not a smooth course going from one stage to the next. Instead, one usually slips backward to a previous phase, moves forward, jumps over and returns to past stages again and again. Each time one reverts to a previous stage, the time spent in that phase is usually of shorter duration as one is usually able to move out of it more quickly. However, the intensity of feelings during this process can continue to take your breath away in pain.

Many grief experts have identified phases or stages of normal grieving to explain unwelcome loss and to give a framework for identifying tasks and feelings experienced in the process. There is a major criticism of the stage models of grief in that "stage models" do not adequately address the idiosyncrasies of individuals that impact grief. The stage models imply a progression from one stage to the next in an orderly fashion. Grievers do not, however, always progress through the grief process in an orderly fashion. Grief is an experience that is far from smooth and orderly. It is confusing, unpredictable, painful, and yet a healing journey.

## WORKING THROUGH LOSSES

The experience of working through loss is a complicated series of operations which can be characterized as a process or journey with tasks to be accomplished at every step. Understanding this process is an integral part of the journey. Feelings of confusion and chaos cloud understanding and cause fear in the grieving person. As educators and mental health counselors, we need to be familiar with the grief experience so we can give hope and direction to the clients and families we serve. We are the ones who will help them make sense of the chaos they are experiencing and teach them skills needed to learn to live with their losses.

Loss can be anticipated or sudden. The intensity and duration of the grief will vary depending on whether there are opportunities for comprehending the grief, such as in anticipatory grief. In any case, grieving is a series of operations with unavoidable non-linear passages.

This next section will give an overview of how people grieve.

Every griever will follow this process in some form, in one's own time frame and with one's own emotional accompaniment. There is no one way that every person grieves. The common denominator is that each person experiences pain. So while each experience is similar, it is totally unique to the griever. This is an excellent illustration of why grieving people take umbrage with well meaning comments of "I understand how you feel".

## PROTEST

To protest is to resist or object. In grief, protest is a resistance or objection to the death or loss. It is not a denial but it is a way of disbelieving, of pushing the full impact of the loss away until such time as the grieving person is more able to fully comprehend it.

Thus, after an unwelcome loss, the first step of the experience is to protest it, to resist believing it. The intensity of this stage and the way it is experienced have much to do with whether there was warning of the loss with time for anticipation, or whether the loss was sudden and unexpected. If it is sudden, the stage of protest can be more intense. Initially one experiences a sense of unreality, shock, numbness. Grievers use words of disbelief and denial in that this experience cannot be real, and they voice true objections to the loss.

Accompanying this protest, there is often confusion, absent-mindedness, a sense of unreality, and haziness. Wandering around the house, forgetting things, ending up in one room and wondering why you are there are common experiences. Anxiety may begin to penetrate the body and physical symptoms appear, such as dry mouth, tightness in chest or throat, hollowness or nervous stomach. Sleep and appetite disturbances often appear. One may feel a need to get up and walk aimlessly about. The body is mobilizing itself as if for an emergency. Yet the bereaved may feel numb, physically ill, and angry as well as disbelief. There is a part of the self that is saying "this is a bad dream, and I will wake up and find everything is back to normal". The mind of the griever is totally preoccupied with trying to grasp the reality of the loss.

This protest of an unwelcome loss is an inability to accept the reality of the loss. Denial and mental distancing are the mind's way of distracting attention from the loss in order to get a brief respite from the pain of grief. Our body and mind are so interconnected that in grief, there are times when the mind protects the body from experiencing the intense pain of the loss by the defense mechanism of denial.

These responses can be relatively short-lived, sometimes lasting for hours or days, or sometimes weeks. Most people do not experience strong emotions during this time, with the exception of *anger* and *numbness*. When the anger is directed inward, the feelings of *guilt* are generated. The most common sensations are a feeling of numbness and a sense of unreality.

Anger is a surface emotion, often driven by other intense and sometimes disowned feelings. Look beneath the anger and see what the emotion is that may be driving the anger. Is it fear or hurt or guilt? Does the person feel abandoned and rejected by God or a Higher Power? If they ask why this happened to them or what did they do wrong, why do they feel sad and frightened by losing someone or something they have relied upon for protection, and why did their lives have to change, the grievers are trying to gain some insight about the loss. In the grieving process, these questions and emotions of protest are natural. When they are acknowledged and validated, they can frequently be lessened and somewhat obviated.

Remember that this process and these feelings can apply to situations other than death. As stated above, rape victims, abuse survivors, children of divorce, children of addictions also ask questions such as above.

## SEARCHING

Searching is the process of trying to connect with that which is lost, trying to understand the loss. As the numbness and unreality of an unwelcome loss gradually begin to wear off, a grieving person begins the searching phase. This is a difficult time for both grieving people and those who are around them. Thoughts become obsessive for the griever. Thoughts come into mind at random and without provocation. This thought process can be compared to a video tape that keeps on running in your mind, a preoccupation, which cannot be turned off. Part of the mind is truly searching for that which is lost, thinks that the lost may still be found, and yearns to return to the time prior to the loss occurring. In small children, this may be a time of regression to more infantile behavior, a time when one felt safe and secure. This searching phase reflects the total disruption of the griever's life and psyche.

This phase absorbs a tremendous amount of psychic energy. It often is surprising and angering to the grieving person that the rest of the world can still function "as usual." Anger, at almost anything, is prevalent when one is searching for that which is lost. This is understandable; someone or something has been taken away—often we cannot identify the anger or we try to suppress it, only to find it bursting forth in unexpected times and ways.

People, when searching for the person who has died frequently wear clothing of the deceased, smell the deceased's perfumes or aftershave scents, visit grave sites, listen to music that was shared between themselves and the deceased, and constantly think about the deceased. This is done in an attempt to connect somehow with that person who is gone. It is a time of horrific feelings of loss, abandonment, grief, physical pain, and overwhelming sadness.

It is difficult for the grieving person when in the searching mode to look at other lives, seemingly normal and unaffected, without hurt and resentment. Searching is a time when we are looking for answers to often unanswerable questions of "Why?" and "Why me?" "I need to understand and make some sort of sense of this nightmare. Help me understand why." This is an exhausting time due to the intense preoccupation in trying to make sense of the feelings and pain of the loss. Searching is emotionally and physically draining for both the griever and for those friends and family close to the griever.

Inherent in searching for a lost person or thing is that of re-evaluating one's identity. "Who am I?" "Where do I fit?" "Where do I belong now?" "What happened to my family? We are no longer a family." There is a searching to find new connections. The family unit identity is forever altered by the death of a child. How do parents respond now to the question of "how many children do you have?"

During the searching experience, grievers may pray to the deceased, talk to them, worry about "where they are." The bereaved thinks and hopes the deceased can somehow still be affected by the bereaved person's thoughts and behaviors. Searching is a time of total absorption with the loss and its initial impact.

School professionals will see the searching experience in situations other than death. When professionals tell parents that their child has a developmental delay or mental retardation, the family too go through the grief process. For parents who are told that their child will not follow the typical path in life, they often search frantically to understand the disability. The drive is to become armed with knowledge which might give them a sense of control over something that is out of their control.

## DESPAIR

Despair can be defined as the feelings of sadness and lost hope in the yearning to connect with that which is lost. More and more as the searching fails to bring relief from the loss, the feelings of numbness fade and the pain and reality of the loss become more prevalent. One descends into the most painful and difficult part of the process. Despair is a time of giving up all hope of reconnecting with that which is lost. There is a sense of hopelessness that pervades the mind. Emotions become waves of despondency, anguish, sadness, heartache, aloneness, and yearning. As the waves of the ocean wash over the sand again and again, so too do the waves of despondency and despair come crashing over the griever. The increased awareness of the reality of the loss brings intense pain and immeasurably deep sorrow. However these feelings are not usually constant. The waves of despair and hopelessness are typical manifestations of normal grief reactions.

It is very important to note the intermittent nature of despair in bereavement. In grief, it is natural to experience anguish, followed by periods of relief from the pain. It is basically a depressed state where it is difficult for one to find the energy or interest in anything other than oneself. Sleep and appetite patterns are often disrupted during this phase. When despair is most intense, it is a type of clinical depression in that the bereaved is constant in feelings of hopelessness and helplessness.

Depression as a condition of despair can be situationally caused, chemically induced or caused by a physiological chemical imbalance. Grief is a time of situational depression and the despair experience is certainly a depressing time. Society, through rules such as one is allowed only three days of absence from work for grief, does not allow grievers much time to mourn. Most grievers are not given time to become clinically depressed, as they are needed by their children, jobs, and friends. Thus they may not have the time or the energy to resolve their own issues. Most people want those who are grieving to move on and to return to normal. These attitudes of others can be offensive to the griever and may even exacerbate the feelings of loss.

Despair lasts much longer than most people want to believe. For example, four to fourteen months after the death would be within the normal range that despair can be expected to occur. Most people expect one to be back to normal within six months, yet at six months, the difficult period of grieving is just beginning. People can be helpful to those who are in grief by understanding the length of time that the feelings of despair are likely to last. There is *no* set length of time for the despair process journey, nor can one build a bridge across the valley of despair in order to avoid its agony. Not allowing oneself to feel despair does not cause the feeling to dissipate. Instead, despair is merely put aside temporarily only to surface later with more complexity, intensity, and difficulty. The only way through despair is to experience it, to feel the sadness and loneliness, and to "give despair words". Expression of the despair is important for it lets grievers know that they *will* eventually overcome their feelings of hopelessness and this will allow them to mobilize and move forward with their lives.

## REORGANIZATION

Another phase of grieving is when grievers begin, usually on an intermittent basis, to experience hope. Reorganization is a time of learning to reorganize one's life around that which is lost. At intermittent intervals grieving individuals begin to express interest and enjoyment in life, along with plans for making changes in their lives, i.e. they begin to reorganize their lives. It is the time when hope of the lost being found is relinquished. Such reorganization, however, is a period of draining work, fatigue, apathy, and at times, hope. With a death, life becomes disorganized and desperate. Reorganizing to overcome despair is trying to learn to live with the empty chair or bed. It is a beginning, not an ending. It is the slow start of a new identity, a new way of life. It is growth but it is painful, slow, and difficult.

One valued outcome of grievers beginning to reorganize their lives is the recognition that life *must* go on, there is a glimmer of hope and it is acceptable to think of a new life. It is the beginning of the adjustment to having lost someone or something that has caused the grief. The loss still hurts. And there will be painful acknowledgment and recognition that life will never be the same— and it won't be. There is sadness with a smattering of hope.

## REINVESTMENT

The reinvestment experience is an end phase of grieving. However, remember the experience is not a linear process so a grieving person may continue to revert to one of the above phases at any time. Reinvestment is a time when there is the conscious willingness is to let go of the past and to focus on the present and future, without the loved one. At this point, grievers are willing to commit to relationships, to work, to past and new interests, and to establish and accept their new identities. Reinvestment does not mean forgetting the loss, but remembering is no longer quite as painful. One of the biggest fears of grievers is that their lost loved ones will be forgotten. The fear is justified as other people do forget, while grievers never do. The loss experience is etched in the griever's mind forever.

The reinvestment phase of grieving is the beginning of new relationships, reduced suffering, and different thoughts about the self. It also may be the beginning of forging new bonds with a loved one who has died or with a relationship that is lost. It is not "getting over the loss", it is learning to live with it, with the accompanying empty chair, the empty bed, and the savage hole in your heart. It is part of the healing process.

One important concept must be restated: Grieving will not cause one to completely forget one's loss. ( As a griever, one of my greatest fears was that everyone would forget my beloved husband and it would be as if he never existed in their lives. This has not happened. Others have forgotten the date of his death and many things about him but they have not forgotten him. As a griever, while I think of him daily, they do not. They do not live with the constant reminders of him and of his absence.)

In the case of the death of a loved one, the healthy outcome of the grief process is to derive strength from the loss and to incorporate this strength into a new life. With this new life comes different relationships with that which is lost. This strength is necessary because the grieving process requires hard work if healing the suffering is to occur. Time does not heal grief. Grievers do the work.

Loss must be digested intellectually. "I must somehow make sense of his death, understand why . . . ." Then it must be realized emotionally. Emotional tolerance begins when the bereaved no longer feels the need to avoid certain reminders of the loss for fear of being flooded by pain, remorse, and grief. This is exhausting work, as the griever must review every element of the loss in order to begin to bear it emotionally.

The bereaved person must make a new model of self and the outer world change to match the new reality, a world without the deceased in it. This is known as "learning to live with the empty chair." Frequently, the empty chair includes a new identity, from Mrs. to Ms., to not being called Mom or Dad by the deceased child, and with that new identity, which has been involuntarily thrust on the bereaved, comes a whole new set of assumptions about one's own self. This compounds the confusion and sense of chaos and loss.

In short, the bereaved's tasks are physical, emotional, intellectual, personal, social, financial, totally encompassing. Perhaps this helps the reader understand that the resolution of grief involves a process, a growth process, a painful yet healing process, a time-consuming process, but by no means an event with an assured beginning, middle, or end. In fact, there are times during the grief experience that it feels as if there is *no end* to the pain, the problems, or the process.

When training school or agency personnel on the topic of grief, I have no prior knowledge of what the audience's individual experiences have been with death and I do not want the workshop to turn into a group therapy session for a selected few. Thus I use the analogy of a person losing a wallet or keys as a teaching strategy for the stages of grief described above.

Think about it: You have just discovered that you have lost your wallet or your keys. What do you say? After the most common response of some expletive, you probably say, "No, I could not possibly have lost it. It must be here . . . I could not have been so stupid to have lost it . . . ." This is the *protest* phase. It is a denial of the loss. We protest things every day of our life. Did you protest getting out of bed this morning?

Then what do you do? You look for your wallet or keys. You search with the intent to find that which is lost". This is your main task in the *searching* phase. It is a way for you to understand what led up to the loss, what caused it, and what you need to do to try to fix it. It involves obsessive thinking about the loss, like a video over which you have no control.

After searching all over for your wallet and not finding it, you begin to think about the contents: photos, credit cards, license, Social Security card, and the sentimental items that were in the wallet and you may feel a sense of *despair*. It may seem overwhelming to think of trying to replace these items, as you may not be able to restore the photos of your loved ones and other items that were in the wallet. But what can you do? You must move to the next stage and *reorganize* around the loss. You replace your wallet, get a new license, Social Security card, and credit cards. You find new photos, and you organize your new wallet. Obviously, this analogy does not begin to portray the intense feelings of despair felt with catastrophic losses but this metaphor is a great teaching tool.

You have a new wallet but there is often a lingering thought that you *will* find that wallet somewhere, someday. You are able to withdraw the emotional energy that went into the preceding stages and *reinvest* that energy in the present, as it is, without your lost wallet. But do you truly "accept" the loss? Treatment of addictions requires that one ACCEPT he/she is an addict/alcoholic; grievers may find "acceptance" a difficult word to use here. Grievers learn to live with the loss but that is different from accepting it.

This analogy is easily applied to persons who are attempting to deal with their grief and after going through protestations, searching, and despair, they begin to reorganize their lives and function in the present, while they continue to remember and to love the missing loved one. They are invested in the present as it is, with an empty chair, living life fully but with total awareness of their loss.

The most well known beliefs about the nature of the grieving process were set forth by Elizabeth Kubler-Ross (1969), over three decades ago. She asserted that there were five stages of grief. She referred to these stages in the grief process as **denial** and **isolation, anger, bargaining, depression, and acceptance.** An assumption in her approach is that grievers go from the first stage, in a linear fashion, to the last stage. These stages, known as **DABDA**, are used today in work with terminally ill patients. Many terminally ill patients do come to an acceptance of their impending death, while their families may not. The Kubler-Ross stages are also germane for the addictions and spinal cord injury fields. It is imperative for the recovery process that spinal cord injury patients, addicts, and alcoholics go through each of these stages, in a sequential manner, in order to come to an acceptance of their conditions.

Acceptance is a term commonly applied to addiction recovery and deserves some attention here. In addiction work it is known that one must honestly accept the fact that "I am a compulsive overeater or alcoholic" in order to really embrace the recovery process. Remember, addiction is a disease of denial, delusion, secrecy, and most importantly, perception. The process of acceptance for addiction utilizes Kubler-Ross stages, from denial to acceptance.

The word "acceptance" is a difficult word for survivors of loss. Parents who have survived the death of a child find it hard to accept the death. It is easier for a child to learn to live with a divorce rather than to have to accept it. People reinvest in life without the loved one far more easily than having to accept the finality of the loss, as evidenced by the loss of the wallet analogy. For persons who have experienced a traumatic loss of a loved one, there is no acceptance of the idea that their loved one is gone from their mind. So as a member of the helping profession, be aware that the definition and interpretation of the word "acceptance" may differ from griever to griever and loss to loss. It might be an important distinction and have different applications based on the client's definition of the term.

As we examine the consequences of grief, please recognize that the function of the grieving process is *not* to sever all bonds with a lost person. It is to begin new attachments. Too often one hears survivors say that friends and family tell them to move on, get over the death and get back to the way they were. Develop new relationships . . . that will make you feel better . . . kind advice but not helpful. This advice may cause a dilemma for the bereaved. They can feel as if they are wrong or crazy for grieving and mourning. They might already feel isolated from others. When they feel that they cannot return to "normal", they may withdraw further into themselves and their grief.

Grief is not a psychological state that ends and from which one recovers and returns to "normal." It is a process, a growth and healing process, that one must travel and often more than once. This concept must be stated and understood by all mental health and education professionals who work with grieving people!

Grief resolution tends to focus on the formation of a continuing and evolving bond with the deceased. This means that total disengagement from the past and the deceased does *not* characterize the result of successful mourning. Continued attachment with the deceased used to be considered unresolved grief. More recently, another model of grief proposes that bereaved survivors want to remain involved and connected to their deceased loved ones. They actively construct an inner representation of the deceased that changes with time. Young children, for example, often think of their lost loved one in a certain portrayal, even fantasy, but that representation changes with time as they grow, develop, and become more cognitively mature.

Robert Anderson, author of the play "*I Never Sang for my Father*" said that although the death of his wife ended her life, it did not end their relationship. This is such a truism! Relationships continue in survivors' minds as they try to work toward some resolution or comprehension of what was taken from them. A cognitive understanding of the loss often means peace for the griever. Some might say it is an acceptance, but others might say it is learning to live with the hole in your heart.

Those who lose a loved one with whom there was considerable attachment maintain that connection through their conversations, dreams, thoughts, mementos, and memory. They even try to mimic them by using phrases that the lost loved one used. They try to keep them "alive" in some way. As stated earlier, they may talk and pray to them directly. They may allow their lost loved ones to have some influence over their present lives.

Some people say they feel as if their loved one is watching over them—and they had best behave. (After my husband's death, my daughter commented that now Lee could watch her *all* the time, so she had better behave!) Thus, while the intensity or character of the relationship with a lost loved one may diminish over time, the relationship itself does not disappear—and most grievers do not want it to do so. Memories become treasures!

Grievers tend to believe, perhaps with validity, that everyone else's lives are going on "normally". While others usually forget the anniversaries, birthdays, and special moments of their deceased loved ones, the grievers do not. And there is a certain amount of anger one often feels when others don't remember and are unaware of our pain. (When the tenth anniversary of my husband's death occurred, I felt hurt and angry that, other than my children, no one acknowledged it. My daughter put the feeling into words, saying that "sometimes it is hard to recognize that everyone else's life is going on normally while in ours we miss him every minute". Out of the mouths of babes come such truisms!)

Grieving involves the processing of one's thoughts and emotions within various social contexts over extended time. The suffering (that is grief) may end but the loss is seldom forgotten. Depending on the intensity of the grief, the loss will be forever remembered. The grieving person is never the same again due to the need to accommodate to shifting self perceptions and changes in all the contexts of one's life. It is absurd to ask anyone "to get over" an intensely felt loss.

Never again, it should be noted, will the contexts in which the grieving occurred be the same. Where grieving occurred in the family, school, work setting, or friends, the character of these settings, particularly as perceived by the grieving person, will have been changed. In short, both the person grieving and the environment where the grieving occurred are altered.

Accommodation allows us to incorporate the past into a larger whole in the present. In this process, the griever seeks to comprehend the meaning of the loss—past—into the context of the present life. It occurs over time and with acceptance of the reality of the loss.

# The Experiences of Grieving and Growth

## This experience is painful, unpredictable non-sequential, and essential for grief resolution.

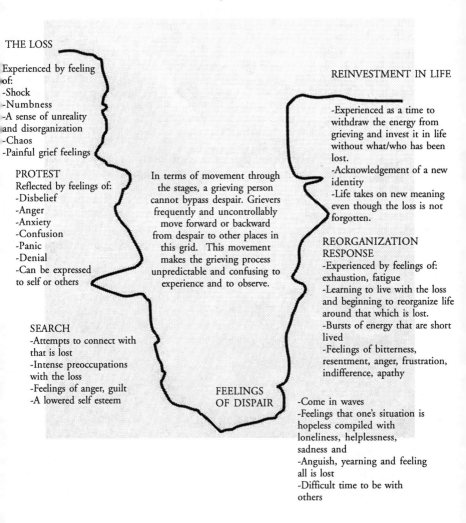

**THE LOSS**

Experienced by feeling of:
-Shock
-Numbness
-A sense of unreality and disorganization
-Chaos
-Painful grief feelings

**PROTEST**
Reflected by feelings of:
-Disbelief
-Anger
-Anxiety
-Confusion
-Panic
-Denial
-Can be expressed to self or others

**SEARCH**
-Attempts to connect with that is lost
-Intense preoccupations with the loss
-Feelings of anger, guilt
-A lowered self esteem

In terms of movement through the stages, a grieving person cannot bypass despair. Grievers frequently and uncontrollably move forward or backward from despair to other places in this grid. This movement makes the grieving process unpredictable and confusing to experience and to observe.

**FEELINGS OF DISPAIR**

**REINVESTMENT IN LIFE**

-Experienced as a time to withdraw the energy from grieving and invest it in life without what/who has been lost.
-Acknowledgement of a new identity
-Life takes on new meaning even though the loss is not forgotten.

**REORGANIZATION RESPONSE**
-Experienced by feelings of: exhaustion, fatigue
-Learning to live with the loss and beginning to reorganize life around that which is lost.
-Bursts of energy that are short lived
-Feelings of bitterness, resentment, anger, frustration, indifference, apathy

-Come in waves
-Feelings that one's situation is hopeless compiled with loneliness, helplessness, sadness and
-Anguish, yearning and feeling all is lost
-Difficult time to be with others

# CHAPTER 4

## TYPES OF GRIEF RESPONSES

This chapter outlines come of the responses to loss. These are divided into typical responses and then some complex responses. Physical reactions, confusing thoughts, somatic complaints, and changes in concentration are typical responses to a grief experience.

## TYPICAL GRIEF RESPONSES

**Grieving persons often express their loss experiences in the following terms:**

Feeling numb, robotic in reaction

- Anger
- Fear
- Sadness
- Guilt
- Anxiety
- "Hit by truck"
- Confusion
- Feeling physically ill, tired, drained, exhausted
- Feeling as if out of control
- Feeling overwhelmed
- Feeling lost
- Out of body sensations

**In response to the loss, grievers' thoughts can be:**

- Disbelief, denial of the loss
- Confusion, an inability to concentrate
- Preoccupation about the loss experience like a video tape, over which one has no control, constantly running
- Hallucinations of the lost person
- A sense of unreality as in "He'll be coming back—this isn't really happening"
- Time distortion—seems like the event occurred yesterday and years ago simultaneously
- Out of control, scattered, fragmented
- A sense of depersonalization, a feeling of "I am not really here" while the thinking process tries to contradict that sense with a more reality based thought

**Physical responses to grief can include:**

- Hollowness in stomach
- Nervousness in stomach
- Tightness in chest
- Breathlessness
- Hypersensitivity to noise
- Hearing their heart beating with loud "thuds"
- Being prone to somatic illnesses, feeling sick
- Appetite disturbances
- Sleep disturbances

**Behavioral responses to grief can include:**

- Sleep disturbances
- Eating changes—food doesn't taste good
- Wandering aimlessly
- Social withdrawal, isolation
- Day and night dreams of the missing loved one
- Avoiding reminders of the loss

- Searching/calling out/visiting places
- Treasuring objects, letters, photos, mementos
- Becoming fixated on reminders of the loss

## ANTICIPATORY GRIEF RESPONSES

Anticipatory grief allows us to absorb the reality or the fantasy of a forthcoming loss gradually. Developmental losses, such as children leaving home for college or retirement, give us time to prepare for the event—and sometimes we actually look forward to the milestone. We prepare for the loss by completing unfinished business, by making plans for the future, and by trying to gain a sense of control over the impending changes.

Parents who know that their unborn child will be born with severe and/or life threatening defects have an opportunity to undergo anticipatory grief. When a couple is told their unborn child has a terminal birth defect such as anencephalia and will die soon after birth, the birth parents can begin the grief process prior to the birth/death of the child. Anticipatory planning might include the naming of the child, the planning of the funeral, taking photographs, inviting family members to the hospital, working with clergy or grief counselors, and deciding on family memorials. This anticipatory planning gives the family a sense of control over a devastating event.

Anticipatory grief may be present during the latter stages of a chronic or terminal illness and provides the mourners with a pre-death grief preparation. The survivor can anticipate the death of a loved one and with that knowledge, can have the opportunity to discuss previously unspoken issues and emotions; and work toward positive closure. This pre-death grief is likely to impact the nature, course, and duration of the bereavement process. Many times grief therapists help clients do this. The comment I have heard over and over again sounds like this: "How very grateful I am to have had the opportunity to say all that we did. I feel at peace with there being no unspoken feelings."

Perhaps to further understand loss, we need to mention separation anxiety. Death is the ultimate separation for both the dying person and the survivor. The threat of separation tends to elicit enormous anxiety, fear, and a struggle to hold on to life. It is a normal process but one that should be acknowledged. If we work with this separation fear by planning how the deceased will be remembered, it can reduce some of the fear of loss. This can also make the grief process easier to comprehend when the death actually occurs. Anticipatory grief gives the griever a chance to begin the separation and adjustment process before the final loss occurs.

There can be adverse consequences if the grief work is done too effectively and the anticipated death does not happen. There can be ambivalent feelings in the griever when an anticipated death does not occur. A woman was diagnosed with terminal cancer and given a very short amount of time to live. Everyone at her job said goodby to her at the end of the school year, in anticipation of her not returning to teach the following September. When September arrived and she was back at her position, some of the faculty did not know how to respond to her. In their confusion, they distanced from her which made her feel guilty at being alive! Family members often say to me "I wish (s)he would either die or get well because this is just too hard on me! I cannot put my life on hold forever . . . ." This are not insensitive reactions. They reveal some authentic and important feelings, and are elements of anticipatory grief.

Anticipatory grief can occur in advance of losses other than developmental or death. For example, when patients are to undergo mastectomies, they often speak to others who have recovered from such procedures and found ways to cope with their loss. Positive attitudes assist healing greatly, and anticipatory loss discussions can allay fears and offer hope for survival and recovery.

There are five aspects involved in anticipatory loss that are based on the first task of mourning: to understand and accept (there's that acceptance word again!) the reality of the loss:

- One must acknowledge that the loss is inevitable and this acknowledgment does not come easily. I cognitively knew my husband's death was going to occur quickly and although I appeared to be fully cognizant of this fact, emotionally I was not prepared.
- One must be allowed expression of the physical, emotional, and interpersonal turmoil associated with the loss, and it is a roller coaster of feelings! Give sorrow words.
- There must be the development of a perspective on the loss that preserves the worth of the loss as we, the grievers, want to understand it. We want to give the loss some sort of meaning. This is a cognitive process related to searching to understand the loss.
- There is a rational detachment that permits your cognitive and affective domains to function separately. Your head and heart think and feel a lot and sometimes there is a need to separate them due to the pain of each. The pain of both sometimes is too intensely agonizing.
- Recognition of what is going to be left behind and proactive ways to memorialize the loss can offer a proactive stance rather than a reactive one. I often ask terminally ill clients how they would like to be remembered by friends and family and how to plan for some meaningful memorials ahead of their death. Many terminally ill clients leave videos or journals for their children to view and/or read at developmental stages of their lives as anticipatory ways to be remembered. It is important for us to feel as if we will not be forgotten once we are deceased. Anticipatory grief offers opportunities of control to the terminally ill patient and family members to preserve significant memories which encourage the continuing bonds of connection.

Losses such as relocation to a different geographical location, an impending leaving home for college, or an upcoming marriage can be incidents for separation anxiety and anticipatory loss.

# UNRESOLVED GRIEF RESPONSES

### Absent Grief Responses

In absent grief, the grieving person shows no emotion, pretends life has not changed, or is not permitted to express feelings of grief. Feelings of grief and mourning are seemingly absent. This may be "a strong, silent person." This means the griever is either in denial of the pain of the death or in the stage of shock. The inability to express feelings of sorrow and grief is not a healthy reaction. Absent grief often surfaces years later. It may manifest itself in other forms of clinical symptoms such as depression, anxiety, eating disorders or addictions.

### Inhibited Grief Responses

Inhibited grief is a lasting inhibition of showing the signs of grief, but often with signs of other symptoms, physical or psychological, in their place. I have heard many grievers say they were not allowed to show their sadness, that they had to pretend it was not felt and function as if life were "normal." This type of grief differs from absent grief as the signs of grieving are not permitted. They are present and deeply felt but kept within the griever. As with absent grief, inhibited grief responses can lead to later problems.

### Delayed Grief Reactions

Normal grief may be delayed for a period of time, perhaps due to more pressing responsibilities or to the griever's being unable to deal with the pain of the loss at that time. If there are multiple losses that occur within a short time, the bereaved will often delay mourning the most painful one. It is too painful to mourn several losses simultaneously. However, a trigger event later can bring on a full grief reaction, and the griever feels truly overwhelmed, devastated, or as if "hit by a truck."

## Conflicted Grief Responses

According to grief expert and author, Therese Rando (1984), in conflicted grief there is an exaggeration or distortion of one or more of the indications of normal grief, while other aspects of the grief may be forgotten or suppressed. An example might be the death of an alcoholic parent, where the relationship between the parent and the child may have been ambivalent and conflict ridden. Problems could occur in the emotional acceptance of the loss due to the complexity of emotions felt by the child toward the addicted parent. This grief can be abnormally prolonged.

## Responses to Unanticipated Loss

This occurs after a sudden, unanticipated loss and is so disruptive that recovery is usually complicated because the grievers have difficulty understanding the full implications of who or what they have lost. As Rando says, "their adaptive capabilities are seriously assaulted." Events such as the World Trade Center disaster and air plane crashes can bring on this type of grief. This type of loss is exacerbated when the bodies are not found as the bereaved have no tangible evidence of the loss to assist them in the cognitive process of understanding the reality of the loss.

## Prolonged Grief Responses

Prolonged grief responses occur when grief extends beyond a typical three to four year duration and there is no lessening of the intensity of the pain. The bereaved cannot see or feel any progress or growth in the grief process. The chronic griever continuously manifests intense grief reactions that would be seen in the early stages of grief. There is high risk for possible pathology, substance abuse, eating disorders, and other self-destructive behaviors in attempts to deal with or avoid the intense pain. An example of prolonged grief could be an adult whose sibling died during childhood yet whenever the death is mentioned, the pain of the loss continues to be so intense that the adult weeps uncontrollably.

**Disenfranchised Grief Responses**

This type of grief response occurs when someone experiences a loss that he/she does not or cannot openly acknowledge. Because it is not known publicly, it is not socially supported. Disenfranchised grief may occur because the relationship is not recognized, such as ex-spouses, same sex relationships, and some step-parent relationships. When the loss is not recognized as being significant, as in perinatal deaths, abortions, pet deaths; or the griever is not recognized, such as the mentally disabled, very young or very old persons, the griever is left out from being supported or is disenfranchised. I spoke with a female whose best friend, a male and not her husband, died. She did not feel she could openly grieve because no one really knew how close the two friends were and she was fearful that people would suppose a relationship other than friendship.

**Stigmatized Grief Responses**

This type of grief is complicated by the mode of death and how the death is interpreted and reconciled within the bereaved's frame of reference. We interpret events and develop meaning from our experiences within our own personal constructs or beliefs. Our belief systems are already challenged by a death, and we must learn to adapt to the loss. If the death is by AIDS, drug overdose, capital punishment, police action against a criminal, or suicide, the societal stigma and blame actually impede the bereavement process. Feelings of shame, guilt, embarrassment may be felt by the bereaved and may stifle expressions of mourning, thereby complicating the grief process. The bereaved may not receive the usual recognition accorded survivors, leaving the mourner to grieve in silence and isolation. The loss of social supports due to societal stigma is one more factor which may impede the grief process.

# INDICATORS OF COMPLICATED GRIEF

One clue to complicated grief is when the person cannot speak of the deceased years later, without experiencing intense and fresh grief. Tears and pain are normal responses during the first years of the grief process. The experience can become complicated if it continues beyond three or four years. An exception to this time frame is the death of a child where, due to the intensity of the loss, it is not uncommon for a parent to well up with tears several years later. If parents continue to treat the deceased child as if he/she were still living, or show resentment toward the living children, this is complicated grief.

Students who have suffered the death of siblings often have complicating factors in their grief experience. Sibling grief is difficult to talk about with parents as it can trigger parental sorrow and the surviving child feels guilty doing so. Survivor guilt or the feeling that "I should have died, not my brother" is another complicating factor for youth. The movie "Ordinary People" offers examples of complicated grief and survivor guilt. Students whose siblings have died are often overlooked by school personnel once the death is out of the limelight. Friends, some extended family, and school personnel may forget the loss over time, and in doing so, expect the bereaved person to be fully alert and functioning academically, athletically, and socially. This just does not occur. Bereaved students who have experienced sibling or parental death need special consideration for a full four years, if not longer. Thus sibling grief issues frequently do not get resolved and often complicate later life.

Another clue to complicated grief is when, years later, the person is unwilling to move any material possessions belonging to the deceased, even enshrines the deceased. In the early stages of grief it is common to want to keep possessions of the deceased in tact. If it continues into the later years, it may be a sign of complicated grief. For example, parents who ten years later continue to keep the bedroom exactly as it was when their child died are expressing an unwillingness to acknowledge the loss and to move on. This does *not* mean that you cannot keep the blanket that your late grandmother made you ten years ago! Memorabilia of the deceased is a way of continuing bonds with the missing person. It is when there is rigidity in the maintenance of the memory that it may become complicated.

If a bereaved person develops physical symptoms similar to those the deceased experienced before death, this can be a clue to a complicated grief pattern. Remember it is normal to be concerned about developing the same symptoms, but most of us do *not* develop the same conditions or remain fixated on these physical symptoms. Youth often fear that they too will get the disease that killed their sibling or parent. They may manifest similar symptoms but they should not obsess over them. When children and youth experience death, their immune system often reflects that loss in that they tend to get sick easily. That is different from contracting the same disease that killed their family member. And they may need to be shown the difference.

When the bereaved person makes radical changes in his/her lifestyle, it could be a sign of complication. It is recommended that if possible, no major changes in lifestyle be made for at least a year following the death of a spouse. Sometimes financial or health pressures necessitate radical changes and that is not a sign of complication. How the child or adult reacts to that radical change is telling, however.

When a student presents a long history of subclinical depression, often earmarked by persistent guilt, sadness or lowered self-esteem, that history is a clue for potential complication. When a child has a pattern of mental health adjustment issues, counselors and school personnel must be vigilant for complicating clues and early intervention opportunities.

When a student exhibits a compulsion to imitate the dead person, that can be an indication of complicated grief. Commonly, survivors feel the need to "carry on" what the deceased started, but soon that need dissipates. When the bereaved youth seems to try to "be" the deceased, counselors and school personnel must be ready to clarify for possible intervention.

Clear clues of self-destructive thoughts, impulses, and actions may be indicators that the bereaved person wants to join the deceased. Some clients say very clearly that they want to die. Some grievers self mutilate. Listen to their words and believe them. Assess for suicide ideation and a plan. If there is any indication of suicidal thoughts, get help fast. Do not err on the side of trusting the child not to hurt himself or on the implementation of a safe behavior contract. Research has shown that when a person decides to take his/her own life, safe behavior contracts are nothing more than pieces of paper. School personnel must contact parents, supervisors, and immediately refer the child for an outside evaluation.

Unaccountable sadness occurring at a certain time each year and lasting for a time can be another clue. It is normal to feel sadness at significant events such as the anniversaries, birthdays, and developmental milestones the deceased is missing. The sadness is understood, and while it is most intense around the actual date, it eventually becomes bearable. If the sadness persists for extended times around the significant dates and it has been four years since the loss occurred, this can be an indication of complicated grief. If the grief reactions have been suppressed, they will surface under seemingly unaccountable situations. Talk with the child or client and see what thoughts, feelings or events might have triggered the seemingly unaccountable sadness. If the feelings persist, refer the student for outside assistance.

Some bereaved people develop a phobia about illness or about death. This can be another indication of complicated grief. If a phobia, an irrational fear, begins to limit a person's life functioning, it is complicated. Counselors and school personnel must be observant for any complicating factor in the grief process.

## TASKS OF MOURNING

Inherent in the normal experience and reactions to grief are the accomplishment of the tasks of mourning, the public display of grief. These tasks, according to J. William Worden, Ph.D.

(1982) are difficult pieces of work that the griever must complete in order to reestablish a sense of balance to one's life. The first task of mourning is to **acknowledge the reality and finality of the loss.** This occurs primarily in the protest and the searching phases. At times the bereaved acknowledges the reality of the loss and yet still expects to see the deceased walk into the room. Young children do not understand that death is final and irreversible and they may expect the lost person to present himself at any moment. They don't understand the meaning of the loss. They may make the loss less significant than it actually is. Some children selectively forget the loss, including what the deceased person even looked like. The process of coming to an acknowledgment that the loss is real and final lasts for a long time. The first year of grief is one of feeling numb and steeling oneself from moment to moment, from significant event to significant event. The second year of grief is when the reality and finality of the loss set in. This is how it is, day to day, without the loved one. Thus the second year is often much more difficult than the first year for grievers.

For students, they are often able to function more effectively for the first year following the loss. But during the second year, grades drop, concentration and focus are difficult and everyone wonders what happened. School personnel must be aware that the second year of loss for students is a time when they often need more attention and assistance academically.

The next task in the mourning process is for the griever **to experience, acknowledge and tolerate the pain of the loss.** Feelings of hopelessness and anguish engulf the griever, leaving him/her feeling as if an ocean wave has swept him/her out into a sea of pain. This period is difficult for both the griever and those family and friends around him/her. It is a time of confusion, anger, fear, sadness, and intense yearning for the lost person or situation. The pain seems unbearable at times and yet the griever must learn to tolerate the feelings. As a wave recedes, so too does the pain eventually. Some grievers may try to short-circuit the pain experience by cutting off their feelings and denying the pain of the loss. Some people try to run from the pain by being constantly busy or by traveling to find a change of venue cure. However, avoidance is not healthy. If this task is not accomplished, the grief process can be complicated and extended.

High school students may try to mask the pain by over-involvement at school, by alcohol and or other drug use, by anger, withdrawal, and/or intense peer social relationships, to name a few. School personnel should be vigilant for behaviors of concern exhibited by students who are in this state of grief.

The third and perhaps most difficult undertaking is **the adjustment to an environment in which the loved one is missing**. Learning to live with the emptiness is painful and takes great readjustment skills. Learning to live in an environment without a loved one entails more than just adjusting to a loss. Often what is actually lost does not become clear right away. The secondary losses complicate the process of adjustment to an environment that lost a parent. This task takes time, effort, and support of extended family and friends. It is a time period that requires tremendous energy and often leaves the bereaved exhausted and emotionally drained. Students who are learning to live in homes where a parent or sibling has died are often unable to concentrate or focus on academics during this time. Educators should be aware that this level of catastrophe devastates a family system. Everything is changed for the child. New roles, new responsibilities, new fears, new stressors, new routines are the norm. Chaos and confusion reign during this time of reorganization.

And the last task is **to withdraw the emotional energy from that which is lost and reinvest it in life as it is now, in the present, without the loved one**. Reinvestment is *not* forgetting the deceased. It is *not* being disloyal to the lost loved one. It is being present in the life that is reorganized after the loss of the loved one. When this task is complete, grievers begin to show increased happiness and reinvestment in their lives and activities. They are more actively participating in school, sports, peer relationships, jobs, and other efforts. Life seemingly has found a new balance for them.

When does mourning end? While there is no ready response to this question, grievers do learn to live with the loss. There are few choices other than to do so. There are certain benchmarks of resolved grief reactions, such as being able to think of a lost loved one without intense pain. Perhaps mourning is finished when the grieving person can reinvest in life as it is without the lost loved one. Terminology such as "end" and "finished" give a finality that most grievers dislike. Grievers rarely forget the person or situation over which they grieve. They do not "get over it" but they learn to adapt to the environment into which they are thrust. They reinvest their emotions back into life without the loss and into the living.

But does the process actually end? For some, it may and for others, it does not. An example of this is a grandmother whose grandchild died at birth. She feels uncomfortable with the continued grief and mourning that her children are experiencing. She does not understand why "they cannot get over it" and let it end. Until she walks in their shoes, she will not understand it and she runs the risk of alienating them if she judges their grief to be aberrant.

# CHAPTER 5

## THE CONTEXTS
## IN WHICH GRIEF OCCURS

### DETERMINANTS OF GRIEF RESPONSES

There are several factors that can influence how one will grieve. The grief process is an individual experience yet there are some commonalities that affect the path of grief. It is important for counselors and school personnel to understand what factors influence the experience of grief, especially for children. These determinants of grief responses include:

- The importance or value of the loss as perceived by the child, adolescent, or adult. Who the person was in the life of the bereaved student, and the roles played by the deceased or lost person as well as by the survivors are key factors in determining the grief response. Relationships that are ambiguous or dissonant can have a more negative impact on the person's response to loss.
- The age of the deceased and of the griever are important. Young, unexpected deaths of children cannot be easily understood or rationalized by adults or peers. The death of any young person occurs out of sequence in the developmental life cycle. This change in sequence is very impactful in the resolution of grief. Many grandparents

say they wish they were the ones who had died as their deaths are more in the proper sequence of life events.

The developmental stage of a bereaved child at the time which the loss occurs is a determinant of the child's grief response. Children who are nonverbal cannot understand the loss the way a child who is age 6 can. Thus, the chronological age and maturity level of the grieving child for whom any catastrophic loss occurs are essential determinants of their response to the loss. Children can comprehend divorce or death and their impact only according to their age, maturity level, and degree of cognitive development and understanding. For example, young children who experience loss may not understand the finality of the loss due to their "magical thinking" cognitive level. Older children and youth make sense of the loss differently as they have greater cognitive functioning skills. Developmentally delayed youth will respond at their own level of cognition, which may be more reflective of a young child due to the developmental cognitive delay or level.

- The nature of the attachment to what or whom is lost, especially the degree of ambivalence, conflict and dependency within that attachment, are determinants of grief responses. A younger child who is very attached to a parent will have a more difficult separation than a child whose degree of closeness is more ambivalent. However that degree of ambivalence can also be a source of guilt which can confound the grief process. Conflictual relationships can be difficult to resolve, again, due to the degree of guilt that a grieving child might feel. I worked with a young man whose gym teacher died suddenly. This child had argued with the teacher the day prior to his death and was convinced he had caused the death due to the conflict they had experienced. Thus, discussion about any felt guilt is critical to the grief resolution process.

- Childhood experiences with other losses and how the losses are discussed and experienced impact the grief process for children. Loss is cumulative so the way we are taught to experience early losses has an impact on how we will acknowledge and accept future losses. The death of a pet is a valuable learning experience for a young child. Well meaning parents who buy a replacement pet stunt the grieving process for the child. Children need to know that one cannot replace a lost loved one, even a pet. This loss experience with pets will teach children how the next loss is to be faced.

- **How** the loss occurred is important data. Was it sudden, preventable, accidental, violent, or precipitated? Was the mode of death considered socially acceptable? With the kidnaping situations so public, young children are being exposed to the terror and violence that a kidnaped child and parents must endure. Losses like kidnaping may have a major impact on surviving children in fear of it happening to them. If the loss is divorce related, was there "justifiable reason"? In divorce, adolescents tend to assess blame on one parent in an effort to understand the reasons behind the loss. Some parents feed into this blaming by slandering each other. It is truly hurtful for any child to hear one parent slander the other.

  *Remember*: **Criticism of one parent is criticism of one half of the child.**

- Personality variables, especially those dealing with the expression of feelings and tolerance for pain and anxiety are determinants of grief responses. Some students are verbally expressive of feelings and loss while others are loathe to identify or discuss their feelings. It makes them too vulnerable. Never assume that a student wants to talk to you about their loss experience. Many do not!

- Social, cultural, religious variables, including rituals and precedents are influential in grief reactions. My father's death was easier for me and my children as we had experienced my husband's death sixteen months earlier, and precedents or rituals for grieving had been established. We knew what to do and expect, so the chaos and confusion were less. Also the relationship between the children and their grandfather differed from that with my husband, which is another variable in the grief process responses.

- Secondary losses or stresses that are occurring simultaneously impact the grief response, such as concurrent bereavements, unresolved bereavements, children at home to care for, illness of the survivor, or financial pressures. A student may experience several losses simultaneously, especially following a major loss crisis. The grades may drop, the child may be cut from the athletic team, there could be peer losses in relationship breakups, and/or parents could be in the process of divorcing with a resulting relocation necessary. It is common for there to be several secondary losses following a significant loss for an adolescent. All of these losses and stresses occurring together make the grief process very difficult and confusing for the student. This places the adolescent highly at risk for maladaptive behaviors, and educators and counselors must be exceptionally observant for any concerning behaviors. Students often think in terms of extremes such as "always" and "never". Thus when they feel overwhelmed, their extremist thinking can offer few options or behavioral choices to them. This is a time when they need assistance in breaking these stressors down into more manageable pieces, clear education on what to do to diffuse the feelings, and acceptable behaviors to express their pain.

- Social support systems are essential in the determination of healthy grief work. Isolation is common but not healthy. Grievers need close relationships that can support the grieving person in positive ways. Too often supportive people feel they must push the griever to "normal". This is not support. Supportive systems allow the expression of grief in positive ways and in the griever's time frame. Supportive helpers do not offer advice or criticism. They encourage, they listen, and they are present for the griever. This is a difficult job as grieving people are not easy to be around. Grieving is a roller coaster of emotions, with little predictability in feelings and behavior. Children may appear happy and carefree one minute and in tears the next. Supportive systems recognize this unpredictability and assist the griever by providing the consistency of support to the mourning person. For some grievers, having other obligations such as a job, children, or school forces them to focus on something/someone other than themselves and their feelings of loss. Schools should be excellent support systems for students. Unfortunately most school personnel are uncomfortable dealing with loss issues and that discomfort is communicated clearly to the grieving faculty or student. School systems need to be trained in the process of grief and how best to support grieving students and staff. Support systems cannot be minimized in their role of assisting grieving adults and youth.

*Remember*: **Grievers often say "Wherever I am is not where I want to be; thus I roam around trying to find that person who is gone from my life."**

• Knowledge and participation in the death and the funeral processes are often significant in how one will grieve. With the World Trade Center/Pentagon/Pittsburgh disasters, it has been clear that finding any remains of the deceased aids in acknowledging the loss. Remains of the deceased prove that the person is dead. Without that knowledge, grievers have more difficulty really believing that their loved one is gone. With children and youth, **accurate** knowledge and **appropriate** participation in the process assist them with the tasks of mourning. Children should *never* be forced to do anything they do not want to do at a funeral. They should not be forced to touch the body or look closely at it. Forcing behaviors like that can leave scars that remain forever.

- The continued presence of supportive figures in the bereaved's life is itself a positive indication of how well grieving persons will manage their bereavement. **Continued presence** is the key part of this indicator. Often there are numerous support systems initially but over time, these friends and family members return to the normalcy of their lives. Grievers' lives must learn a new sense of normalcy, and they frequently feel abandoned by support systems. Continued presence for counselors and school systems means observing students for behaviors of concern, drops in grades, isolation from peers, withdrawal from activities, and changes in attitude for several years following a child's major loss.

It is imperative to remember that school personnel and counselors, friends and family can help people cope with loss, but *cannot* and *should not* try to do it for them, nor should they try to help them avoid the pain. Grief is a painful, yet healing process through which growth can and does occur. For such growth to proceed among grieving people, they must be given the opportunity and a safe environment in which to grieve healthily.

## GRIEF IN THE FAMILY

Loss impacts the family system in numerous ways. Losses that are stigmatized by societal reactions may have deeper repercussions on a family's ability to re-balance itself. A parent who goes to prison, an addicted parent, a suicided family member, a drug overdose death are examples of stigmatized losses. Losses due to death by non-stigmatized circumstances, going to war, divorce, relocation, or normal developmental stages are more readily discussed and acknowledged by the grieving parties, thereby making the familial adjustment easier. When the loss is marked with disgrace, there is another factor added to the family's already long list of adjustment tasks.

Educators and counselors must understand the impact of loss on a family. This is especially true when the loss is totally unexpected. This section, while on the family system, should be helpful for mental health professional and school personnel in comprehending the devastation that an untimely death or loss has on an entire family.

Families are systems, with the behavior of one person affecting the behavior of everyone. A traumatic event such as death, rape, addiction, divorce has ramifications of each person individually and on the family system as a whole. The paradigm in family therapy is that the whole is greater than the sum of its parts. Thus to overlook the impact of grief on a family system would be reprehensible.

Premature death forces families to face the developmental tasks of the life cycle out of their planned sequence. An example of this is when a child predeceases a parent or a parent dies leaving small children to face the developmental stages of their lives with a substantial void. Children are not supposed to predecease parents. Parents are not supposed to die until their children are grown. When a young parent or a child dies, the gradual, expected course of the family life cycle is inextricably altered. The family is challenged to absorb the reality of the loss, with its many emotional and practical implications, into the already demanding work of growing up together as a family.

Loss is a deprivation experience and as such, it redirects the course of family development and becomes interwoven with the family's developmental tasks. Grief is a deeply shared family developmental transition which involves a crisis of attachment and a crisis of identity for family members. While the family members experience the same loss, each feels its impact individually. It is this unique experience that is most difficult to share with other family members. In addition, each family member has his own idiosyncratic skills of coping with the tragedy. The different grief coping modalities can be irritating to different family members, especially if one behavior is in direct opposition to someone else's manner of grieving. Grief and its ramifications are even more difficult for students to share with teachers, school counselors, or other helpers. Youth barely understand normal adolescent feelings and they are truly confused with grief feelings.

It is important to recognize that death interrupts the normal course of life for the family and redirects it. The family struggle is how to absorb and integrate the loss so as to reestablish the stability needed to resume the family activities in what is believed to be their normal growth process. This is a difficult task as it is usually unchartered waters with no previously developed course of action to follow.

The loss of a valued family member creates a crisis situation. Family members attempt to adapt consciously and unconsciously to the emotional cues of other family members as they try to understand and control their own emotions. This is an effort to get back into a pattern of living, and in this process to construct a new sense of identity. Society puts pressure on families to do this quickly as most businesses give three days leave for grieving and schools are pressuring students to resume their academic obligations so as to "keep current" with their work.

Thus, grief within the family creates a crisis of both attachment and identity.

For example, children, adolescents, and adults manage grief in ways that are based on their individual aversions, attractions, and explanations. Children cannot understand concepts that are beyond their cognitive capabilities. Adults may initiate a period of withdrawal from others and retreat into a private reality within which the enormity of the loss can be gradually felt, acknowledged, and life rebuilt.

For children the unremitting pace of adult grief is just too intense and too painful. They are not cognitively able to follow the course of most adults. Thus they are more likely to cope with moments of distancing coupled with moments of longing and intense preoccupation with the losses. Both adults and children integrate the emotional reality of death in the family gradually, in ways they can cognitively manage and that do not totally overwhelm their capacity to cope with the requirements of daily living. This is a tough task for all! In addition, grieving adults are often emotionally unavailable to their grieving children as they are so overwhelmed by the magnitude of their own feelings and obligations. This leaves youth alone to try to comprehend their grief feelings. This is a time when counselors who are knowledgeable about the process of grief are invaluable.

As stated, grief is difficult to share. Each of us has our own personal way of dealing with our problems and feelings. There are gender differences in emotional reactions. Stereotypically women express their feelings frequently, while men are problem solvers and "fix-it" personalities. Death, loss of a parent to prison, war, addiction are not fixable experiences. Loss is a time of chaos and feelings of pain, helplessness, and powerlessness. It is a time when the differences in emotional expression can become sources of conflict, misunderstanding, rejection, and loneliness. Since each person had a unique relationship with the loss, each person will have will have his/her own way of grieving that loss. Remember, there is no one correct way to grieve, so when spouses or children suffer the same loss, such as the death of a child or a parent, each family member will grieve in his/her own way. Some people, children or youth, will want to talk about the deceased constantly, while others may prefer a more silent introspective means of mourning.

It is essential that we recognize and allow for personal differences in styles and expressions of grief. Because a child or loved one does not express feelings and anguish outwardly does not mean that this person is not in excruciating pain. Feeling hurt, broken, and very alone, the expression of these feelings is unique and individual. However, counselors and educators must be alert for unhealthy responses to loss. When grievers do not express their feelings openly and their behavioral responses seem aberrant, helping professionals need to intervene.

To reiterate, it is critical for healthy family bereavement that everyone, family members and professionals alike, recognize and respect the differences in grief reactions and coping styles. Sharing one's grief experience, feeling understood and responded to by other family members, and reestablishing a coherent sense of the family's past, present, and future are just some of the essential and formidable tasks for the family to accomplish in recovery. When families shut out shared grief, the loss of access to one another can compound the losses associated with the death and contribute to a profound sense of isolation.

In short, a family's first priority in managing the crisis of grief is to reestablish the equilibrium needed to support ongoing family growth and functioning. This effort is lifelong and especially critical at certain family developmental functions, such as graduations or weddings. The family will never be as it was; thus the process of establishing growth-enhancing stability while integrating a new sense of identity is an enduring challenge. This challenge is confounded by the normally ever-changing development of the family system.

The timing of family bereavement will vary with the degree of stress and gaps in the circumstances of the loss. The greater the degrees of stress and discontinuity, the greater the need for growth-controlling structures that mitigate the overwhelming aspects of the grief experience, reestablish stability and further restrict disequilibrating change.

Over the course of the family life cycle, families continue to integrate the reality of the loss and its consequences on the redefinition and reorganization of the family identity. Each unchartered stage of family development initiates new realizations of the loss while providing opportunities for growth by integrating some of the previously avoided or splintered aspects of grief.

Changing family relationships will include adjustments in the relationship with the deceased or missing loved one. Specifically, this change dilemma is evident in the response to the question "How many children do you have?" posed to parents who have experienced the death of a child. The relationship appears altered, and yet the bereaved wants to retain the relationship, wants to treasure its every moment. One father explained, "I just say I have four children: one in Washington, one in Colorado, one in New York, and one in Heaven." He maintains his relationship as father even with the deceased child.

It is important for families to reintegrate the deceased into the family as an evolving, spiritual presence whose image continues with the family's developmental growth. Grieving families fear the deceased will be forgotten and want to keep some form of relationship with the missing person. One does not, however, continue to set a place at the dinner table for the deceased!

Families with incarcerated loved ones or with mentally ill family members face a similar dilemma in telling the public. Stigmatized loss is difficult to explain for fear of public disdain. Thus maintaining a relationship with this loved one poses problems, especially for adolescents.

Very slowly, over months and years, the reality of the loss is acknowledged and integrated into ongoing patterns of living. For this author, it is not an acceptance, but it is learning to live with the loss. Part of learning to live with the loss is knowing that friends will forget and move on with their lives and that they will have no understanding of the major life transitions the grieving family undergoes. But friends, family, school personnel, and mental health professionals need to know that it takes many years to achieve the reconstruction of lives and identities when families, have suffered the loss of a significant person. Lives are inextricably altered, patterns of daily living splintered, inner emotions are set into turmoil, and relationships are significantly affected.

To stress a point, educators and counselors need to understand that while children and parents may grieve together, the loss affects each individual uniquely and the expression of grief is unique to the individual. The grief reaction of each person will be shaped by the needs and reactions of the others in the family. In this systemic process of shared grief, the parental reactions will often provide the leadership for what children will be able to express and understand. This is especially true in the divorce loss. The reverse will also be true in that bereaved children's emotional reactions and relationships to their grieving parents will also affect the adults' bereavement experience.

A brief word on remarriage: Remarriage to a person whose first spouse has died can be difficult for the new spouse and any children. Living with a ghost can be very difficult. The deceased has a history that the new spouse, and perhaps children, cannot be a part of and toward which the new spouse may feel competition. Often the deceased is glorified and it may seem that the new spouse will never be fully integrated into this pre-formed family unit. These feelings of being an outsider may be felt and expressed by all members of the family, most often the children, making for discomfort and resentment. Reassurance and clear communication help normalize the inherent difficulties in the integration process and can assist in diffusing blended family tensions.

Children rarely ask for a replacement parent. If you are the "replacement", do not think it will be an easy transition for you. Take it slowly. Never revile the deceased. Give everyone time to build a relationship with you and you with them. When you criticize a parent (dead or alive), you criticize half of the child.

## UNDERSTANDING GRIEVING PARENTS

This section is included to help school personnel and counselors understand the death of a child from a parental perspective. As a counselor or teacher, you may come in contact with parents who speak of a deceased child often. It may seem as if they talk too much about a child who may have died years earlier or even as a stillborn. Educators and counselors need to understand the deep impact that losing a child has on a parent, which of course impacts the living children and other relationships within the family system.

Losing a child is the most dreaded loss and truly catastrophic.

Stillborn babies, babies who live for a few hours or days, and miscarriages are often mourned silently for years. The mothers who carried these children grieve intensely and many times silently.

Often this grief is misunderstood by others and the parents are expected to "just get over it. This attitude diminishes the connection between parents and deceased child. Society hurts parents by not fully recognizing the intensity of the parent/child bond, regardless of the number of hours the child lived.

I know mothers whose children were stillborn and who have these births represented on mothers rings or on cherished charms symbolizing their births. No matter what the age of the child when he/she dies, there is a lasting imprint of love within parental hearts. When parents commemorate a child's life, even if that life was mostly intrauterine, it was still very significant to those parents. In speaking about this book with a colleague, she told me her story of losing two sons, soon after their births. These deaths occurred at least 25 years ago and as she spoke of their births and deaths, she quietly wept.

Child death is a loss that cannot be diminished. In truth, one can never replace a child. We are blessed to have them for any amount of time. When a child dies, parental grief continues for years. That grief resurfaces at every symbolic developmental stage where the child's absence is keenly felt. For example, when a deceased child's academic class graduates, and the child is obviously absent, the pain of the loss resurfaces with incredible intensity for the family. This is a time when schools often contact the parents, telling them of a memorial moment or a yearbook page dedicated to the memory of their child. This helps grieving parents feel their child has not been forgotten by the school or by classmates.

Please acknowledge that the life of a child, regardless of duration, truly exists for the parents and let parents grieve openly. Schools can help grieving parents, siblings, and friends by recognizing the importance of memorializing the lives of these deceased children.

# UNDERSTANDING
# GRANDPARENTS' GRIEF

When a grandchild dies, the grandparents suffer a dual loss. They grieve the loss of a precious grandchild but they grieve for their adult child's suffering too. The helplessness that grandparents feel in not being able to help their child or their grandchild is overwhelming. A grandchild's death seems totally unnatural as it defies the natural order of life. Children and grandchildren are not supposed to predecease grandparents.

Do not assume that, because grandparents are a generation removed, they are immune to the intense pain of such a loss. Do not assume that grandparents are any more experienced in the loss process due to their advancing age. Do not assume that they will not need as much consideration and support as the parents of the deceased child. Do not assume that grandparents will "know how" to cope with the devastating loss of a grandchild.

Because grandparents are usually not responsible for day-to-day care of a grandchild, they are often spared from the usual conflicts between generations. This plus an increase in leisure time often makes it easier for grandparents and grandchildren to develop a closer and more unique relationship. Many grandparents invest hopes, dreams, even financial resources in their grandchildren. Mary Lou Reed, author of *Grandparents Cry Twice* (2000) states that a grandchild represents the grandparents' immortality, their legacy to the world, one generation extended. Thus, losing a grandchild leaves the grandparent struggling with a grief process where they wish they were the one to die.

## UNDERSTANDING CHILDREN
## AND THEIR RESPONSES TO DEATH

There are many misconceptions about children and how they grieve. It is a misunderstanding that children will complete their mourning quickly. First, let us abandon the word "complete," as grief is a process, not an event. It is not about getting over it, it is learning to accommodate to a whole new world without someone special in that world. It is clear that if a child loses a parent, there is no way the child's life can be reconstituted as it was before the divorce or death. And if a child loses a sibling to death, jail, addiction, the child often loses both parents to grief. This will be discussed later. But to assume that children complete their mourning quickly is erroneous.

Research has helped teach that children who have lost parents to death continue to maintain relationships to their parents by feelings, memories, fantasies, and behaviors that brought them closer to their deceased parents. [This is often true with children of adoption as well.] One child brought a picture of her deceased mother to her kindergarten class Show and Tell. She proudly stood there and introduced her classmates to her deceased mom. A difficult moment ensued as complete silence followed her disclosure. No one knew what to say to this child. Sometimes self-disclosure leaves a canyon of space between the recipients of the disclosure and the person who disclosed, with resulting feelings of "why did I ever tell them?" Children of loss truly feel that they are different, which prolongs and exacerbates the pain of the loss. In the example cited above, when the child returned to the circle, looking downcast, an adult asked the child softly if she needed anything. The child looked at her and said "Yes, I think I need to cry". The adult gently asked if she would like to leave the circle and sit on her lap. The little girl did so and wept.

The inner representations or portrayals of a child's deceased parents change with the maturity and development of the child. These inner constructions provide children with comfort and a connection to the deceased. They help facilitate the pain of the loss at the child's rate of adjustment.

The Child Bereavement Study, sponsored by Harvard Medical School's Department of Psychiatry at Massachusetts General Hospital identified five types of activities children use to maintain connection with their deceased parents.

One activity is *locating the deceased parent*. Many bereaved adults and children want to know where the deceased is. "I want to know Daddy or Mommy is safe . . ." The most common concepts are of heaven and "knowing where my loved one is". This creates a sense of relief and peace for the bereaved. Many children and youth believe the deceased person continues to have animate qualities, and can move, hear me, see me and watch over me. This may explain why some grieving family members are drawn to psychics, channeling, and mediums such as John Edwards.

Another activity is *experiencing the deceased* such as feeling that the parent is watching them. This can be a connection as with a special event ("I believe my dad is watching me as I graduate today"), or it might be associated with a fear or unease that the parent might not approve of what the child was doing. "I had better behave because Dad is watching me."

Children *reach out to the deceased* by visiting the cemetery, writing to the deceased in a journal, letter, or poem, or talking to the deceased. These are ways of feeling connected with the absent parent. They might wear the clothing of the deceased or sit in the deceased's chair or even sleep in his/her bed. The searching to connect with that which is lost is ongoing.

Reflection and memory keep the deceased parent present in the child's waking thoughts. *Waking memories* are often literal reflections of events shared with the deceased parent. These recollections keep the deceased connected to the child. If you lost something very dear to you, you too would treasure the waking memories of events. That is the purpose of photographs, letter, or journals.

*Linking objects* are ways to have something tangible that belonged to the deceased. This is another means of connection or searching to connect with the deceased. Wearing clothing of the deceased, viewing pictorial collages of shared times, listening to shared music, and treasuring possessions given by the deceased are all linking-object activities. These transitional objects may change in meaning as the intensity of the loss lessens or they may retain their significance for many years. Handing down family treasures might be an example of linking objects that have significance for years beyond the loss.

Children's responses to death are often different from the responses of adults. They may not cry or begin to ask questions until months later. Because death is so painful for children, they may stay in a state of emotional denial for quite some time. Frequently, this state of denial is negatively reinforced by adults when they say things such as:

> "You are the man of the house now . . ."
> "You must take care of your mother now."
> "You must be strong."
> "You should be happy because he or she is not suffering any longer."
> "Do not cry . . ."

These things should *not* be said to children. They put unwarranted pressure on the bereaved child. Children need to emotionally distance themselves, to become numb, to gather enough strength to bear the pain of the death. This emotional distancing can take four to five weeks, or even longer for very young children, following the death. Unfortunately, when children finally are ready to express themselves emotionally, the supports are often not there. Be aware that grieving children and youth need your support for a long time after the death has occurred. It is not a constant need, but when a child is ready to express those painful emotions, be available and allow the child to do so. Learn to listen and reassure as honestly as possible. Do not try to "fix it" for the child. Children need to develop their own healthy coping skills.

Children need to be a part of a death in ways that help, not frighten them. They need to share in the tears and the grief, be able to mingle with the family, and attend the funeral if they choose. By being a part of their family's sadness, they receive comfort, support, and frequently adjust more quickly. Exclusion only adds to their feelings of confusion, fear, and isolation. They need clear information about the loss but at their individual level of comprehension.

Remember that children can understand the finality of death only according to their individual cognitive level and ability. If they are very young, their cognitive skills are limited and understanding the reality of the loss will take a longer time. One child, who was four when her father died, began to realize she was different from her friends when she was in fourth grade and the other kids were celebrating Fathers Day and she was not. That was a true realization that her father was really dead, and it occurred years later.

## DON'T TALK, DON'T TRUST, DON'T FEEL

There are three rules commonly associated with children of addictions: don't talk, don't trust, don't feel. When living in a chemically abusive household, it is an unspoken secret that what goes on there, stays there. Children do not trust, as promises are always being broken due to the unpredictability of the drinking, drugging, gambling or other behavioral addictions. Children steel themselves against feeling the pain of broken promises, shattered dreams, and of never knowing what actions are coming next.

In a similar vein, grief is difficult to share, painful to bear, and agony to feel. The bereaved quickly learn that friends and family want them to feel better immediately as they do not know what to do or say to make them feel better. And in reality there is little they can do or say unless they can reincarnate a loved one! In their discomfort, well intentioned friends and family members push the bereaved to move on, to get back to normal, to deny the pain of the loss.

Grievers learn to stop talking about their grief for fear of upsetting others. Children are especially tuned into the grief reactions of their parents and soon learn to keep their sorrow within for fear of upsetting Mom or Dad.

For grievers, trust is diminished whenever there is an untimely loss or death. Questions surface of "Who will die next? Will it be me? Will it be Mom? What will happen to me if Mom dies? What will happen to my children if I die next? Fears come surging forth. For children and for many adults, the assumption that one's world is safe and secure is totally altered and assaulted by a major loss. For many, this assumption of one's world safety was brought to test by the World Trade Center/Pentagon/Pittsburgh disasters of September 11, 2001.

The journey of grief is a journey of feelings. It is a journey from *pre-loss organization* to *loss disorganization* to *post-loss reorganization.* No matter how much academic training this author had in the grief process, I never imagined the pain of my husband's death to be so intense, unpredictable, at times so constant, or the grief work so difficult or so long lasting. Some of the feelings continued to surface years after my husband's death. The intense sorrow that I felt when he wasn't present to share the excitement of major events shocked me. Feelings like these are not easily shared with others, as they tend to be misunderstood or the bereaved feels guilty at feeling them. Happy events, such as the marriages of children, are often sabotaged by the griever's attachment to the pain of the loss. Some grievers may actually feel guilty or disloyal to the missing loved one if they have fun at happy events. Rest assured, these feelings are typical and not aberrant, yet it is permissible to participate at these events with a full happy heart.

Thus the paradigm of keeping silent about thoughts, feelings, and trust issues is readily accepted by grieving youth and adults. Bereaved people read the unspoken messages of listeners which seem to say "do not upset me as I do not know what to do for you". The grievers, then, do not talk about the loss, they do not trust that loss will not occur again, and they do not want to feel the agony of the pain of the loss. Yet these three rules can sabotage healthy grief resolution.

## CHILDREN AND YOUTH
## WITH DEVELOPMENTAL DISABILITIES
## AND GRIEF

It is not uncommon for family and educators to feel they must protect children and adults with developmental disabilities from life's losses and disappointments. They are judged as being too vulnerable to be told of the harsh reality of a parent's death or even of their own mortality. Because their death education is truly nonexistent, they become totally bewildered and frightened at the disappearance of a loved one. Society also often treats the elderly, the developmentally delayed and disabled and young children as being too fragile to handle the trauma of loss—yet it is essential that people of all ages be able to access the supports needed to understand loss and death. Protecting someone from experiencing grief often results in problems and potential future difficulties in grief adjustment.

When a developmentally disabled person is not told of the loss, he or she will still feel the absence of the parent, the sadness of the family, and be aware of whispered conversations and confusion. As the child or adult is excluded, he/she is kept ignorant of facts one needs to know. While the rest of the family is coming to grips with the loss, the developmentally disabled person is feeling frightened, isolated and lost, thinking, "Something is terribly wrong, but what?"

At times of loss and the resulting confusion, the ordinary routines of everyone, including the child with developmental delays, will be altered. Due to concern about the individual's reaction to the loss, denial of the loss may erroneously seem the best course of action. In reality, the denial may *prolong* the person's searching and increase anxiety which can result in angry and aggressive reactions at a later date when one may not connect the behaviors with the loss.

Developmental disabilities encompass disabilities from mild to profound to multiple. In general, the greater the disability, the less likely the individual's grief will be recognized. People tend to ignore or misunderstand the effects of loss on severely disabled individuals. Some developmentally disabled people will have a delayed understanding of the loss process, especially in the areas of irreversibility and inevitability of death. These are difficult concepts to grasp, but these special individuals can understand with communication at their levels of comprehension and patience.

My sister-in-law was severely afflicted with Cerebral Palsy and mental retardation. When her mother died, I remember her at the funeral service with her family and her favorite aide. She was very much a part of the Church service and aware of the solemnity of the situation. Although she had little verbal communication, it was very evident she understood that her mother was gone from her and she grieved. Her family supported her and included her in their grieving process, giving her an opportunity to grieve with them. Although Barbie had severe communication and mental handicaps, a few years later she was able to tell her aides that she wanted to visit her mother's grave.

Professor Sheila Hollins cites the following recommendations to assist persons with developmentally disabilities in their grief:

- Be honest with, include and involve the disabled person in the rituals being arranged for the deceased.
- Listen and provide support for the disabled person for the time immediately after the death and for the months following.
- Remember the comprehension of the permanence of the death is a slower process for the developmentally delayed, so the person may experience delayed grief.
- Actively seek out nonverbal rituals for the person with the disability to utilize and in which to participate. Counseling picture books can be helpful.
- Respect photos and other mementos that the person with the disability can choose. One of the stages in grief is trying to connect with that which is lost and often a memento from the deceased can make a person feel closer to the missing person.
- Minimize changes in routine, care givers, and accommodation for a period of about a year. This is a recommendation for all bereaved persons.
- Avoid assessment of skills as the period of loss and grief may be a time of regression to a safer, more secure, immature behavior.

- Assist searching behavior to support emotional recovery by going to the cemetery or revisiting favorite places. *Hoarding* behavior may suggest that more of this kind of help is required.
- Support the observance of anniversaries of the loss.
- Seek specialists for consultation if behavior changes persist. If serious grief reactions of aggressive behavior, persistent irritability, mutism, loss of skills, inappropriate speech, or self-injury are noted, refer for consultation.

## DEATH OF GRANDPARENTS, NON-PRIMARY FAMILY, AND PETS

The death of grandparents, non-primary family and pets are very significant for children. Please do not take offense at linking pets with human family. Pets are often true family members and their loss is a large family void. My son had a Rottweiler, named Gibson, who lived with me periodically. He became a "therapy dog", a source of comfort and a "friend". When Gibby died, I felt a huge loss as did many of my clients.

These losses are frequently children's first experience with death and will have a major impact on their cumulative loss experience. Loss is cumulative as how early losses are explained and experienced will lay the foundation for dealing with future losses. Loss is a gain and growth experience when properly handled, perhaps a teachable moment.

When a child mentions the death of a grandparent or a pet, the counselors and school staff should respond with full attention and a response that allows the child to talk and vent feelings. "I am so sorry. Tell me what happened," is such a response. Acknowledge the significance of the death by asking the child to share some special memories of the person or pet who died. Please use the words "died" and "death" with children. Avoid "lost" or "gone to sleep" euphemisms that may frighten or mislead a child.

Reassure and affirm the child that death is sad and can be frightening, but you are available if the child would like to share feelings or concerns. It is important for the child to feel supported at this time, and adults at home may overlook the intensity of the feelings of the children.

While it will probably not be necessary to devote lengthy classroom time to these deaths, it is positive to acknowledge them within the classroom family. With the bereaved child's permission, tell the class what has happened, and if others have had a similar experience, allow a few minutes for sharing, acknowledging, and responding. The classroom family can offer support, structure, accurate information, and companionship during a time when the biological family may be distressed and unavailable.

One teacher told me of a child whose behavior had been especially difficult one day. The teacher said she kept guiding the child back on track but was unable to spend extra time with him during the day. As she put him on the bus at the end of the school day, he lingered on the bottom step of the bus and asked, "Did you hear the storm last night?" She replied affirmatively. He said, "Did you hear the thunder and see the lightening? My dog was hit by lightening last night and killed. I wanted to tell you but I did not know how." No wonder he was upset that day! Poor child was in grief over the loss of his dog. The teacher felt dreadful as she knew she missed important cues in helping him deal with his pet's death. The child was most astute in his last comment of wanting to share the information but not knowing how to do it. Perhaps this is another educational moment for educators to teach children how to share their difficult feelings and events with them. Give sorrow words.

## HELPING GRIEVING YOUTH
## AND THEIR FAMILIES DURING HOLIDAYS

There are many "special days" such as birthdays, anniversaries, graduations, proms, and religious holidays that are difficult days for grieving children and adults. Mother's Day, Father's Day, and significant religious holidays are particularly difficult days for the grievers, as these days symbolize "family" and "togetherness." It is important to allow the grieving child to express sorrow, sadness, and the pain of the loss, especially during these significant events. Sometimes it is appropriate to reassure the child that while it does not seem possible, the grief does soften and one does learn to enjoy these days again—perhaps in a different way by beginning a new tradition. (Christmas continues to be difficult for me as my husband really was the spirit of the holiday. So I have tried to do something differently each Christmas in an attempt to find a new tradition or way to celebrate the holiday. This really is not unlike learning to celebrate holidays after grown children marry and move on to begin their own traditions of celebration.)

Schools need to recognize that there will be many non-holidays that still impact grieving students. Prom time was difficult in our house because my husband was so enthusiastic about prom dress shopping, photographs, and rules! Educators must remember that these events may be difficult for grieving students for seemingly insignificant reasons such as "Dad is not here to see me in my prom dress".

Sometimes the daily reminders of the deceased impact the grieving child harder than holidays. You steel yourself in preparation for getting through a special event, but when the unexpected reminder appears from nowhere, it can takes ones breath away.

### Holiday Guidelines for the Bereaved

- Shop early! It might be upsetting, so plan to shop early when there is less confusion. Go with a friend. Try using catalogs. Relax and do not push yourself! It is okay to avoid hearing Christmas carols, seeing all the decorations, watching "everyone else be together and happy." There will be other years to do that.
- Family get-togethers may be extremely difficult. Be honest with each other about your feelings. Talk about what each of you wants to do for the holiday. Do not set high

expectations. Do only what each person is able to handle comfortably.

- There is *no* right or wrong way to handle the holiday. What you choose to do the first year, you do not have to do the next year.
- Keep in mind the feelings of other family members, especially children. Try to make the holiday as joyous as possible for them. (That does not mean to buy them everything in sight!)
- Be careful of "shoulds." Do what is most helpful for yourself and your family.
- Set limitations. Do what is special and/or important to you. You do not have to do everything.
- Once the decisions are made as to how you and your family will handle the holiday(s), let family and friends know your plans.
- Get enough rest and encourage children to do the same. Holidays are emotionally, physically, and psychologically draining for the bereaved.
- Holidays often magnify feelings of loss of a loved one. It is important and natural to experience the sadness that comes. To block such feelings is unhealthy. Keep the positive memory of the loved one alive.
- Often after the first year, people in your life may expect (and want) you to be "over it." We are never "over it," but the experience of many bereaved is that eventually they enjoy the holidays again, perhaps in a different way. Hold on to *hope*.
- Do not forget: "ANTICIPATION OF ANY HOLIDAY IS OFTEN FAR WORSE THAN THE ACTUAL HOLIDAY."
- Do not overspend financially. You cannot buy your own or your children's happiness.

Holidays can be very difficult for children of addictions. Children of addictions often experience an escalation of parental substance use during the holiday season, perhaps resulting in anger, violence, and shattered hopes. Holidays are times of broken promises and shattered dreams for families with active addictions.

# CHAPTER 6

## CULTURE AND STIGMA

### WHEN LOSS IS STIGMATIZED

Some losses are not recognized or are judged by society as not being worthy of mourning. These are called "stigmatized losses" and are somehow tied, by society, to a person's character. HIV (Human Immunodeficiency Virus) and AIDS (Acquired Immune-Deficiency Syndrome), suicide, and death by drug overdose, loss to incarceration are foremost in this category. When a family member dies from a stigmatized death, many relatives are afraid to state the cause of death because of the stigma attached to the mode of death and thereby to the character of the deceased. Children and youth are well aware of these stigmas which impact how they feel they are allowed to mourn and to express their sorrow.

Death by drug overdose is stigmatized as chemical addiction is not understood by many people. Addiction is a disease, not a choice. No one chooses to become physiologically and psychologically dependent on alcohol, drugs, food, or exercise. While drug use is a choice, the addiction to a chemical is not. When addiction is seen as a moral weakness, the result of poor parenting, or some other judgmental explanation, the grief process is stunted by the negative judgement. Mourners feel they cannot openly grieve. There should be no moral judgment about the modality of the death. Loss is loss.

Loss of a parent to incarceration or to mental illness are

examples of stigmatized loss. Adolescents are loathe to expose family secrets in fear of judgment or possible guilt by association.

# AIDS

HIV and AIDS continue to be accompanied by fear, shame, guilt, misinformation, and anxiety. Victims and family members of HIV and AIDS patients are often faced with painful examples of ignorance, stigma, misinformation, fear, discrimination, and even condemnation. Many people do not have accurate information about illnesses referred to as HIV and AIDS. They may have unrealistic fears about contagion such as one can get HIV from toilet seats, daily contact with a person with AIDS, saliva, sweat, tears, or a kiss. This is misinformation and can truly impact society's reaction to the death. False or misinformation and a negative societal reaction to the death often lead family members to feelings of anger, isolation, fear, of being unsupported, and other discomfort.

The term "disenfranchised grief" describes the grief felt by a person who is unable to publically acknowledge the relationship with a lost loved one and the associated grief that accompanies that loss. An example might be a gay relationship where one partner dies of AIDS and the surviving partner is unable to identify or acknowledge the relationship or openly grieve the loss. Another example is the death of an ex-spouse. Due to the nature and stigma attached to either the relationship or the modality of death, the surviving partner is denied the usual means of bereavement. The partner cannot openly admit or show his or her grief in fear of the societal reactions, which are usually blame and rejection. Therefore the lack of social support forces the grievers to mourn silently and alone. Even care givers of persons with AIDS may feel stigmatized and be accorded "stigma by association."

Children and adolescents whose parent or sibling is missing due to stigmatized loss also experience disenfranchised grief. They are often uncomfortable in openly discussing their loss in fear of judgment, embarrassment or shame. Disenfranchised grief can sabotage the grief experience.

# DEATH BY SUICIDE

The cause or method of death has a major impact on the grief process. When death is seen as preventable, violent, and crossing cultural or societal taboos, the grief process is confounded by shoulds, oughts, what-ifs, stigma, fear, myths, and other misinformation.

A child asked a valid question when the sports writer of a local newspaper wrote a beautiful tribute to a young athlete who died of a drug overdose omitted writing anything about a young girl who had committed suicide. The question posed was "Why is it acceptable to eulogize a drug-overdose death, but not what is deemed a suicide?" When another friend of that same child was thought to have committed suicide, the school principal decided that there would be no written memorials permitted in the yearbook. Although this directive was intended to prevent any copycat syndrome due to glorification of death, it actually impeded the grief process. The grieving students got the message because of the stigma attached to the mode of death that it was not okay to grieve this loss. The family felt judged by the school and ashamed to grief publically. This is not the a message schools want to communicate.

School and outside memorials are written in remembrance of the person, not for the mode of death. Newspapers and other media inadvertently glamorize suicide, and in an effort to squelch that glamorization, it is easy, but wrong, to try to put censorship on the whole event. When a child dies, family and friends need to be allowed to grieve their loss regardless of the modality of the death.

# VIOLENT DEATH

Violent deaths are often difficult to reconcile because of the horror associated with them. Images of the violence may be so traumatic for the grievers that they are unable to think beyond the way their loved one died. Airplane crashes, the World Trade Center/Pentagon/Pittsburgh disasters and the plane highjackings associated with them, kidnaping, and other forms of violent death frighten mourners with all the possibilities of the unknown terror that their loved ones may have had to experience. These nightmares can be so terrifying that they impede the grief process.

Murders that are unsolved are very hard for grievers to resolve. Missing in action (MIAs) soldiers may not be dead and the hope of a lost person being alive somewhere makes the grief process longer and harder to resolve. When there is no body to prove the death occurred, as in MIAs or the World Trade Center disaster, closure in the grief process is more difficult. Some sprig of hope that their loved one might be alive remains in the heart of the griever.

Violence in schools has a devastating effect on students, staff and parents. Schools have usually been safe places but with the increase of weapons brought to schools, this feeling of security has been severely assaulted. Schools have been forced to hire security guards, install metal detectors, and develop stringent weapon policies in an effort to restore feelings of safety and security. Once a school has experienced such a violently assaultive event as occurred at Columbine High School in Colorado, the grief at losing and permanently maiming so many students will last for years. The site will always be a reminder of all those victims who lost their lives and of the horror of the incident itself. The site of the World Trade Centers will again always be evidence of the thousands of people who died either in the airplanes or on the ground, and for all the loved ones whose lives were inextricably shattered by these events.

Generally it takes eighteen to twenty four months just to stabilize after the death of a family member. If the death was a violent one as evidenced by children who have been snatched, sexually assaulted and then murdered, the grieving process can take much longer.

## MULTIPLE DEATHS DUE TO MOTOR VEHICLE ACCIDENTS

Automobile accidents kill numerous students every year. When several students are killed in one accident, schools are the most natural place to turn to for help. Crisis Intervention Teams go into action and counseling services are offered to all students. What school personnel may not realize is that the loss may impact the lives of surviving students for *years* to come. For most grievers, the numbness can last for at least six months. When multiple deaths occur in an auto accident or air plane crash, schools may not see the effects of the deaths on surviving students until the next academic year. By then the school has forgotten to support and monitor grieving students as the teachers and administration are back focusing on academia. It is not unusual for grieving students to become symptomatic academically and behaviorally a year or two following the tragedy of loss.

With accidents where students are killed, the one year anniversary of the death(s) is a highly emotional and significant day. School personnel need to be mobilized to observe students for grief behaviors and be prepared to offer counseling services. Services to remember the deceased student(s) are very helpful for mourning students on this anniversary date.

# CHAPTER 7

## GRIEF IN SCHOOL

### GENERAL GUIDELINES
### FOR SCHOOL STAFF

When loss situations occur in student lives, school performance and behavior are often affected. Deaths of student family members, students, or staff impact the school community and need to be addressed. If schools do not have procedures to implement during times of crisis, chaos will reign. Schools have been faced with some very surprising crisis situations, from a superintendent hanging herself in her school office to a superintendent being arrested for cross dressing and child molestation to weapons and mass killings in schools. These situations are indeed of crisis proportion and need to be preplanned.

When students' lives are forever altered by the death of a parent or sibling, a divorce, an unwanted relocation, addiction, rape, or some other catastrophic loss, there will be behaviors of concern that will most likely be manifest in school. Remember, the reaction to loss is based on the way the child perceives the loss and the maturity of his/her life skills in coping with the loss. The following is a formula offered by Larry Newman, a well respected trainer of Student Assistance Teams, which explains this concept well:

**Life skill deficiency**

+

**Crisis** *as child perceives it*

=

**Behaviors of Concern**

Perhaps the most realistic example of this formula is the child who commits suicide over a relationship that ceases. Students today become very involved in their dating relationships, many of which are sexually active. The sexual activity and intensity of the relationship confound the issues and the adolescents are often devastated when the relationships break up. When children have no coping skills, they feel they have no options other than self destruction. Suicidal ideation or action is clearly an example of life skill deficiencies. Students often just do not know what else to do or where to turn.

This section of this manual will speak to what school personnel can do for students, staff, and parents during and following a crisis situation.

The schools' goals when addressing students who are experiencing grief should focus on 1) acknowledging the loss honestly, 2) allowing students and staff to identify and express their feelings, 3) making parents aware of what educators are doing to help the students, and 4) perhaps providing an outlet for the community's desire to help.

Schools, families, and individuals usually experience death and other major loss situations as times of confusion and of not knowing what is expected to occur next. For schools, there may be few policies regarding procedure during the grief process, and unless death within the school community has been experienced, these procedures may go unused. Schools have *Crisis Intervention Teams* called into action when a crisis occurs. There are, however, schools that may not have had to utilize their crisis teams and therefore have not evaluated their procedures.

There are common characteristics of people in crisis, and these characteristics are frequently mirrored in school systems when they must deal with the crisis of death. Confusion is evidenced by shock, disbelief, and protest (denial). There is often an inability to focus on daily matters as the loss takes priority in the mind. Time becomes distorted, anxiety and fears surface, people search for responsibility or blame, teaching ceases (temporarily), and staff question what to do next. There is a feeling of systemic chaos, confusion, and helplessness. It is the time when a valid plan must be implemented to make order out of chaos. Essential tasks of the Crisis Intervention Team are to provide structure to a confusing situation, to give staff direction, and to keep parents notified of what is being done by the school system.

Schools are generally informed of parent or student deaths by some source other than the bereaved student. The students whose loved one has died are usually absent from school, giving the faculty, counselors, and administration time to develop a plan. However, frequently overlooked are other students in the classroom who may have known the deceased and may be present in school. These students may react strongly to the death but may be overlooked, as their involvement with the deceased may have been more indirect and unknown. There also may be students who did not know the deceased person well but still may have had some memorable, even negative, interactions with the deceased.

When death occurs in a school community, educators and counselors must be aware of students who have suffered losses prior to the most current loss. Loss is cumulative and hearing about the death of another student, teacher, or parent often resurfaces the feelings that students felt with their own personal loss experiences. They may not be friends with the deceased but they will be able to identify with what the deceased's family members are experiencing. The school must be aware of varied reactions among students and faculty and be prepared to offer assistance during this crisis time.

# CHANGES IN BEHAVIOR IN SCHOOL AS A RESULT OF LOSS

Educators and counselors should be alert for *changes* from a state of relative adjustment to:

- Decreased academic performance
- Acting out, aggression, hostility
- Incomplete assignments
- Tardiness
- Poor attitude, anger, apathy
- Inconsistency
- Lack of concentration, poor focus, impaired learning
- Withdrawal, isolation
- Change in friends
- Somatic complaints
- Guilt, depression (anger turned inward)
- Regression, "helpless," dependent, less mature and independent
- Fear: "What will happen to me?" "Will someone else die?"
- "You don't understand" attitude, shutting down and people out
- "It doesn't matter" attitude—self-defeating
- Wanting to join the deceased person—watch closely for this one!
- Feeling different, not belonging, not having a family any more . . .
- Generalized anxiety
- Helplessness and passivity
- Specific fears
- Detachment, shame, guilt
- Abrupt changes in interpersonal relationships
- Radical changes in life attitudes
- Depression and self-harm talk
- Anhedonia or the inability to enjoy what was once enjoyable

# CHANGES IN BEHAVIOR THAT MIGHT INDICATE SUICIDE IDEATION

It is important that school personnel be sensitive to risk factors that might indicate suicide ideation. Remember: not all students who exhibit these signs are suicidal. These risk factors act as prevention and early intervention signals. Some of the below mentioned behavioral changes are similar to the changes identified above. Thus counselors should be the school personnel who meet with the student who is manifesting any of these warning signs. The express purpose of meeting with the individual is to do a detailed assessment of the risk for self harm. While these lists are not exhaustive, all educators need to be reminded of them. It is essential to be alert to all behavior changes in students.

Schools need to have continued professional development designed to increase understanding and recognition of the warning signs and possible precipitating events of suicide. The early warning signs are often identified *after* a completed suicide, too late. In brief some of these signs include:

- Difficulties in school
- Depression, sadness
- Drug abuse
- Sleep disturbances
- Eating disturbances
- Loss of interest in activities, dropping out of activities
- Feelings of failure
- Pessimism about life and the future
- Inability to concentrate
- Preoccupation with death
- Giving away possessions
- Putting one's life in order

There are often precipitating events in the lives of youth that might put them at risk of suicide ideation and gestures. These include:

- Loss of close relationships
- Disciplinary crisis that is taken with extreme reaction
- Loss of status with peers
- Identification with someone who has recently committed suicide
- Legal difficulties, incarceration
- Recent failure or setback
- Recent trauma such as divorce, death, illness, loss of money, relocation
- Anniversary of someone else's suicide
- Fear of major life changes

Most schools have suicide intervention pamphlets, policies and procedures. Please ask your school for this information and become familiar with what your district policies mandate.

# CHAPTER 8

## UNDERSTANDING
## CHILDREN'S GRIEF

Children demonstrate grief reactions **emotionally, physically,** and **behaviorally.** At times one form of response may dominate or you may see an interrelationship among and within these three response forms.

These reactions include:

a. A variety of **physical distresses** such as headaches, stomach aches and somatic complaints.
b. **A distortion of time.** Time seems to stop for them making it difficult to begin new projects. The sense of achievement is most affected with older children. The loss compromises children's receptivity to learning, affects their ability to concentrate, and affects their overall attitude toward learning and the school setting. When preoccupied with the loss of a significant person, time loses all meaning.
c. **Feelings of anger.** Aggression and hostility toward others are ways of coping with the guilt that they are still alive, and for all the "bad" things they did or thought against the dead person.
d. **Regression.** Regression to an earlier, safer, self soothing form of behavior may occur in an attempt to avoid the pain of the present. For example, the child may become demanding and helpless or act like a baby or suck a thumb.

e. **Fear.** Sadness may turn into a fear of what will happen to me? To you? Will you die? This fear may make the child feel totally alone, cry unexpectedly, and be unable to verbalize what the fear is about.

f. **Withdrawal** and loss of interest in daily activities may be seen. Grief takes a lot of energy and is totally encompassing.

g. **Eating and sleeping** disruptions and changes.

h. **Emotional changes.** Emotions always find expression, either in a natural, healthy way that is encouraged and acceptable or in an anomalous way that is forced.

i. **Acting out behaviors.** These usually correspond to a child's age and developmental level. One might see temper tantrums, defiance toward authority, increased agitation and fighting, or pure rebellion. One might also see a total shutdown and inability to function, almost a paralysis.

j. **Time and patience.** The grieving process takes time to complete and is often as long as three to four years. When a young person loses a parent, it is this author's belief that four years is a minimum time frame for youth grief processing. The child cannot be permitted to cease functioning during that time, but expect several years to pass prior to real signs of reinvestment in life without the deceased. Learning to live with that empty chair takes years! Just like learning to live with a new person in the home takes years! Thus it is incumbent on educators to remember students who have suffered losses and monitor them for their entire school career.

k. **Progress and regression.** Children, like adults, work through the grief stages with times of progress and periods of regression. Adult care givers and educators must be ready for times when children have surges of loneliness and encounter experiences that trigger memories which penetrate their emotions, both happy and sad. One must accept the child, not push and intrude but provide opportunities for space, silence, acceptance, and discussion of the child's feelings. Sometimes all one has to do is to sit silently and let your accepting presence be felt by the grieving child.

## CHILDREN'S BELIEFS ABOUT DEATH BASED ON DEVELOPMENTAL LEVELS OF COMPREHENSION

Children understand loss based on their level of cognitive development. Cognitive maturation is a progression from a more simple form of thinking to a more complex way of understanding. This progression is clearly evident in how children of different ages and cognitive levels understand the concept of death. The following is a summary of how children of different ages often comprehend the concept of death. This is helpful for care givers to know as it inherently offers information on what to expect in their grieving process.

*Ages 2 to 5*

Children of these ages begin to understand the concept of death yet they tend to deny death as a natural and final process. They may associate the cause or location of the death with all deaths. If the person died in the hospital, they believe that they too will die if they go to the hospital. Children in this age group have no concept of the irreversibility of death and tend to associate death with sleep or a journey, from which the deceased will return. They may even forget that the person is dead. For this age child, euphemisms about death such as "gone to sleep" may be taken very literally and cause the child to be afraid to go to sleep in fear of not waking up. This explanation is consistent with young children's ability to understand other concepts, such as "no". Parents and educators teach and re-teach concepts until children comprehend them.

Thus, explanations about death for very young children should include the use of analogies with which they are familiar.

For example, a four year old can understand that a toy can wear out from being used and loved. This might be a good way of teaching about loss. Music might be another comparison in that when the music stops, it is quiet, but we often keep the words or music in our mind for quite a long time. We remember. Use of the cycles of seasons along with Leo Buscaglia's story of *The Fall of Freddie The Leaf* can help young children understand the concept of death. When working with young children, just think as they do and that will help you create an explanation that can begin to teach them about loss in an age appropriate manner.

*Ages 5 to 9*

Children in this age group begin to understand the reality and the finality of death, yet have difficulty with the thought that they or those around them will die. They believe if they do not talk about death or someone dying, it will not happen. They begin to see the irreversibility of loss. They may be fearful of their parents' dying. This is the age of "magical thinking" that protects them from what really can happen. "Do not step on a crack or you will break your mother's back" is an example of magical thinking. If the mother's back actually got broken and a child had been stepping on cracks, the child's cognitive level and age of magical thinking might make the child feel guilty as if he or she actually caused the accident.

It is not uncommon for a child to wish a parent dead. Unfortunately if the parent dies, the child may actually feel responsible. This is another example of magical thinking.

Some seven year-olds are very concerned with causes of death such as disease, accidents, or old age. They usually have a serious concern about their own health and bodies. Minor aches and pains can be interpreted by them as potentially fatal. Their world ceases when they get a cut until a Band-aid is applied. They need to know that all illness does not lead to death.

Helping children make sense of death is a difficult task and it must be done on their time frame and their emotional level. A question frequently asked concerns whether children should attend funeral services. Being a part of the funeral can help this age group make sense of the loss, as long as it is explained in ways that do not frighten children. They need to have time to learn and think about what they will see, what is going to occur at the funeral home, and what questions they have about the explanations. Monitor children attending funeral services. It is very possible that even the best explanations might not be what the child expected. Never force a child to be a part of the wake or funeral process.

The World Trade Center/ Pentagon/Pittsburgh disasters taught us some frightening lessons. The media coverage was so intense that many adults and children who watched the television coverage became confused as to how many planes were actually hitting the buildings. Children of this age group, as well as many adults, had difficulty separating fact from fiction. Many people who witnessed the tragedies only on television had severe emotional trauma resulting from watching these sights unfold. This certainly addresses concerns about what children should watch on television. It also brings up the question of how schools should tell children about disasters such as what occurred on September 11, 2001. These are areas for school-home collaboration as parents need to have input on this particular topic.

### Ages 9 to 12

Children in this age group begin to view death as irreversible and personal. They often have a real fear of death. They may believe death is sudden, and they do not know where it comes from. They may fear a painful death, dying from falling or from poison. Yet they may not express their fears or pain verbally unless they are in acute crisis. They fear non-existence and they fear separation, but they try to cover such fears by the use of jokes, by being cynical, or by being tough in attitude. This age group may be more inquisitive about the biological components of death as well as the social ramifications of loss on the survivors. The latter end of this age group may be developing a fascination with horror and the macabre, much of which may be death related. Thus the twelve year old may simultaneously have both a fascination and a horror of the concept of death.

Explanations of death for children ages 5—12 will usually center around questions of "What really happens to the body when someone dies?" Children want to know where the decease person actually goes. If the deceased was cremated, there will be questions around the process of cremation. If there is a wake or viewing of the body, the child may have questions about what occurs in the mortuary prior to the viewing. There may be questions about what happens to the body once it is buried. Speak cautiously. When one explains the concept of death to children of any age, be careful to give only the requested information. Too much information can frighten a child. As a teacher or counselor, ask questions as to what the child's perception is of death. Be careful what you say. Never impose an explanation that may be counter to what the child's parent has given.

Children of these ages may be interested in knowing what causes death. Explanations can be comparisons. One can explain that bodies wear out just as toys or automobiles do. One can explain that illness can wear a body out quickly and leave it weaker and unable to fight for life any longer. Whatever explanation is given to a child, ask questions in attempt to assess the child's level of comprehension of the explanation. Never assume the child heard or really understood all you said.

### Adolescence

This is the stage in which youth experience their greatest concern about separation and non-existence, often more cognitively than emotionally. Adolescents tend to examine the meaning of life and death. Teenagers rebel against, question, explore, create, reevaluate, and intellectualize what they see around them. They can think symbolically. They think they are invincible. These normal teenage tendencies can confuse their thought processes when challenged by the concept of death.

Death is both distant and impersonal for adolescents. It is a major part of the media, movies, MTV, and music. Commercial entertainment aimed at the lucrative teenage market often focuses on death by suicide, drug overdose, tobacco use, and violence. Movies, television and the media glorify death which impacts the adolescents views about death. Life is a drama for many adolescents and they may long for a central role in that drama. Death is seen as tragic but dramatic. It gets a lot of attention.

According to Shaller and Smith in an article on music therapy with adolescents experiencing loss, there are five core issues of adolescent development that are affected by major loss experiences. These issues include:

* trusting in the predictability of events
* gaining a sense of mastery and control
* forging relationships marked by belonging
* believing the world is fair and just
* developing a confidant self image

Influencing these core issues are the adaptive tasks of bereavement and crisis which are:

* establishing meaning of the event and its personal significance
* confronting reality
* sustaining personal relationships
* maintaining personal balance
* preserving a satisfactory self-image
* maintaining a sense of self-efficacy (Balk, 1996)

The core issues of development and the tasks of bereavement exist along a continuum and may be influenced by factors of culture, spirituality, personality, family, and peers. This should give the reader a sense of the complexity for the adolescent of reconciling both the core issues and the bereavement tasks.

Since adolescence is a time when children are psychologically and developmentally moving away from parents, the death of a parent during this stage can create added anxiety of wondering if the parent died loving them or if they caused the parent's death by their behaviors. It can threaten the emerging independence characteristic of the adolescent and cause regression to a less mature state. The impact of parental death on a teenager will depend on the individual stage of development, level of maturity, and support systems available to the teen.

The death of a young person or a friend is sad and tragic. It truly challenges whatever fantasies of immortality may exist for the adolescent. The death of a peer may force a confrontation of one's own mortality with one's belief system, and the adolescent may challenge the existence of God, the ideals of fairness, justice, goodness, and right. This is an essential part of learning to understand the loss.

Funerals of young people are usually attended by many other teens, banding and bonding together to console one another in order to try to make sense of the death. We as adults may not understand their intense mourning or their private rituals. Yet these are their attempts to come to grips with the issues of death and their own invulnerability. They still need avenues of adult support and communication open to them during this vulnerable time.

In helping children of all ages, it is important to assess each individual's strengths, cognitive development, support resources and then assess how much reality can be handled at any particular time. The intensity of the loss and the recovery rate depend on the degree of present attachment or involvement to the deceased, the individual, the personality structure, and the defenses used against the grief, and the support systems available. Schools should be ideal support systems but unfortunately they rarely are. Schools want students to get back to work, to become academically productive, and to focus on events at hand. This is very unrealistic.

## HOW CHILDREN EXPLAIN DEATH

Children's explanations of death are often very logical and concrete. They may reflect things they have heard adults say and then interpreted it in their own form of understanding. Some comments reflect fear, some show how they make sense of a concept that most of them have not yet had to experience. Some of them are wonderfully creative and humorous.

- "When you die, they bury you in the ground and your soul goes to heaven, but your body can not go to heaven because it's too crowded up there already."
- "God does not tell you when you are going to die because He does not want you to be scared."
- "God puts you on clothes hangers until He needs you again."
- "You have to get sick before you die, so I am never going to get sick and I'll never have to die."
- "When you die, you do not have to do homework in heaven unless your teacher is there too."
- "Doctors help you so you will not die until you pay their bills."
- "My grandfather died and then my grandmother died because she wanted to be with my grandfather because they were married for 50 years and could not live without each other."

An example of an older [age 17] child's thoughts on the death of her stepfather are the following excerpts printed with permission from the author, Betsey B.[1].

"I never imagined that anything would ever happen to my family. I thought that we were virtually untouchable. Fate sensed my assurance and the tables were suddenly and unexpectedly turned . . . . My life went from average and routine to uncertain and unstable. It felt like I was standing in a canoe in rapid waters while being

[1]    Bausch, Wendy E. 1990 by written permission 2001

shot at from the shore. Everything was so unstable and I doubted that it would ever be normal again . . . Relationships with friends changed. The intolerance in me became overbearing. Problems that people were so involved with were so minimal compared to what I had to go through. My friends who complained about hating their parents made me resent the fact that they at least had their parents. It angered me that they took their families for granted. In reality, before my dad's illness, I was the same way. I became very possessive of people and things. I was so scared of losing my friends. After all, I had just lost the most important man in my life."

# CHAPTER 9

## SUGGESTED RESPONSES
## OF SCHOOL STAFF

### SUGGESTIONS FOR PRINCIPALS

- Revise school forms to include the addresses of both custodial and non-custodial parents so they may receive all appropriate information about school activities, have access to parent-teacher conferences, and report cards of the student *as appropriate*.
- Develop, with the Crisis Response Team and district administration, policies and procedures whereby the school can obtain information regarding special family circumstances that might impact children's behaviors so as to permit teachers, specialists and administrators to be of assistance and yet maintain appropriate confidentiality.
- Set up at least one staff in-service workshop each year to discuss problems of death, divorce, relocation, and other losses experienced by children and their families. Emphasize the importance of faculty understanding loss as a common life experience. Provide teachers with appropriate opportunities to share information on losses suffered by students from one year to the next. Maintain confidentiality as required by state and Federal Statues. Death, divorce, relocation, and other losses are generally public information and anything that is public information

is not considered confidential. Continue to be sensitive about public information that contains hurtful allegations about students or their family members.

- Make professional help available to families and teachers by redirecting or expanding existing services or by suggesting where grief services may be obtained. Remember that when a student dies, teachers often overlook their own grief feelings as they care for their students. Encourage teachers to form their own support groups to help each other learn new strategies designed for teaching students and themselves how to handle loss.

- Provide child care services for all parents who have to bring their younger children with them while they attend teacher-parent conferences and other school activities. Offer conference and meeting time options that are convenient for all parents. Be aware that many teachers are parents also and may have their own student conferences to attend.

- Hold "parent" or "family" activities, not "father" or "mother" activities. Encourage parent-teacher discussion groups. Sharing concerns can lead to understanding, which often leads to the solution of problems.

- Be willing to work with crisis trained professionals outside of the school. In accord with school policies and regulations of confidentiality, share necessary information and work collaboratively with outside resources. Train school personnel in regulations and limits of state and Federal laws of confidentiality. In times of crisis, bring in proven expert clinicians and speakers to provide assistance to students, staff and families. Have available a current listing of outside resources available to families and schools.

- Do not assume that children who experience a significant loss will necessarily have difficulties in school or react to their losses in identical ways. Be prepared, however, to provide them with support should they need it, which might be years after the loss event.

- Provide support to those teachers who want to deal with loss in their classrooms. Form support groups for children experiencing loss. Encourage school staff to form their own support groups to help them learn new strategies designed for helping students and themselves about how to handle loss events.
- Have school newsletters for parents publish information about support services within and outside the school or the district, brief summaries of articles on loss, how students grieve, and strategies for handling loss situations.

## SUGGESTIONS FOR TEACHERS AND STUDENT ASSISTANCE STAFF

- *Know your own feelings regarding significant losses such as death, divorce and the impact of these events on students.* Decide how important is it for school personnel to know what losses a child has experienced, which children come from single parent families, or which children live with active addiction? Ask yourselves how significant this information is in meeting the student's academic, emotional, and social needs. Does this information change how the child needs to receive instruction? Will knowing a child comes from a chaotic home environment change how teachers or counselors interact with him? These are examples of losses that many students endure. The family structure may offer educators and counselors clues as to what support systems are available to the student outside of school. These leads can help educators identify what supports are needed in school as well. Remember that as students grieve these losses and resulting changes in their lives, they may act differently while in school.
- *Be alert for personality and behavior changes.* Does a quiet child become loud and aggressive? Does a child begin to daydream more or begin to fall asleep in class? Does a child's academic performance begin to deteriorate? Do not

make assumptions about the etiology of these behaviors. Be aware of what is going on in the lives of your students. If you are concerned about changes in their behavior, ask questions.

- *Seek support and information from colleagues and parents.* Establishing rapport with a parent will encourage him or her to volunteer needed information should you notice a change in the child's behavior and attitude. Educators and parents need to work collaboratively in the best interests of the children.

- *Provide time to talk with students and faculty about loss situations.* General topics about family life, loss, and the impact of loss on a family can help all students and staff understand and support one another in dealing with the problems that develop from time to time. Students can understand loss as a daily event and apply this knowledge to learn strategies that can assist them in handling more severe and catastrophic losses. Discussions like these assist school personnel prepare for the inevitable loss situations faced by schools.

- *Encourage your school library to order books for students at different learning levels that deal with the many losses that children and adolescents experience.* Topics include child abuse, alcoholism, love relationship break-ups, organ loss, handicaps, divorce, death, relocation, and many more.

- *Find out custody and visitation responsibilities* (if possible) including who should be contacted for emergency situations. Determine how and what information should be shared between school and home. Be careful. Make sure you follow district policy regarding communication with parents. Be alert for behavioral changes when visitation and parenting transitions occur.

- *Always share with the administration information you have about a family situation that may be related to feelings of serious loss.* Encourage administrators to do likewise as appropriate.

- *Provide a classroom climate of safety in communication and time for students to talk about their feelings.* Let them describe what is happening if they want to, without commenting in a "teacherly," judgmental, or even constructive manner. Being a listener who is trying to understand can be a tremendous source of support, provided it is offered sincerely and realistically. Your role is not that of a therapist but a supportive educator.

- *Do not presume anything.* A significant loss for some children may actually improve their home life or it may create a disaster, the effects of which may not be observable until years later. The effects of loss will be quite different for each child.
- *Learn about children's age appropriate grief reactions* and when reactions become a concern.
- *Do not be afraid to ask for help.*

## SUGGESTIONS FOR SCHOOL COUNSELORS, SOCIAL WORKERS, AND PSYCHOLOGISTS

- *Create loss topic groups for students.* Divorce, Death, Moving, Step-parent families, as well as the topic of loss in general, such as the loss of a wallet, sneakers, or library books. The goals of these groups should be educational and skill building rather than therapeutic.
- *Offer to do in-service or staff meeting presentations for school personnel.* Explain to them the stages of loss and what to expect behaviorally and emotionally from students who have experienced losses. Provide suggestions for what they should and should not say. Help them understand they cannot "fix "the losses for the children. They must *not* lower their academic expectations for students in grief. They must, however, understand the process and be ready to adjust academic assignments. They must not try to be a substitute parent for grieving students. They must remain clearly in their professional role in school.
- *Offer to come into their classrooms to teach about loss.* There

will be some staff who will be reluctant to conduct group activities about death with students. Help them to deal with those everyday mini-losses of students so that when the students experience the more powerful losses, they will have a better understanding of what and how to handle their experiences.

- *Suggest books that can help the bereaved with their own losses and the losses of their children.*
- *Present parent programs on different issues about death and loss.* Suggest how parents can respond to their children and work effectively with the schools when children have experienced loss. Make sure that you are knowledgeable and well prepared. Suggest concrete programs, activities, and practical information. Do not overwhelm them.
- *The best way to handle death is to do so directly.* By dealing openly with death, you can help the bereaved heal faster. When any bereaved person is enabled to avoid dealing with death, it is a disservice. This is because it does not help them learn the skills they will need in the future.
- *It is important to accept the feelings students have toward death,* including anger and guilt. Stress the importance of the bereaved's strengths and successes. Having survived so far, some resources must be present. Turn loss into gain by pointing out that they are learning and growing, albeit painfully.
- *Be aware of all the variables that are affected when a death or loss occurs in the life of an adolescent.* Secondary losses are changes that result from the primary loss or death. They are often not obvious but they are painful. Examples of secondary losses resulting from a parental death include a loss of routine in the family, loss of financial security which could put pressure on the adolescent to seek employment or change higher education plans, or the loss of identity as a family. Other adolescent losses which have resulting secondary loss might be when a student does not make a sports team. The secondary losses might include a loss of status or of a team peer group.
- *Know the resources for dealing with death that are available*

*to school personnel, families, and students.* Do not be afraid to suggest outside groups, religious resources, or agencies who can offer opportunities to work on grief issues.

- *Encourage teachers, administrators, and friends to write a note of condolence to the grieving child.* Encourage them to follow the note with a phone call or a visit to the family at a later date. Thoughtfulness during bereavement will have a positive impact. Students remember when teachers attend wakes, memorials, and funeral services or when any condolence is received.

- *Design appropriate reentry programs for students returning to school after a significant death has occurred.* Grief is a process, as stated before, and the bereaved are usually somewhat numb for several weeks following the death of a loved one. Their grief behavior may not be noticed until weeks, months, and even years later. Please do not stop being sensitive to the signs of grief that death has caused.

- *Do not expect the same grief reactions from all persons who grieve a similar death.* Each person will react to death in his own way.

- *Never judge in a negative way the grief reactions of students.*

## SUGGESTIONS FOR ALL SCHOOL STAFF WHEN THE FOCUS IS ON DEATH

*Know your own feelings about death.*

- How has the death of a loved one affected you?
- How has this death affected the way you deal with students' losses?
- Are you comfortable talking about death?
- What makes you uncomfortable about the topic of death?

   ***Seek out the person for whom death is a concern.*** There is a tendency to avoid people who are touched by death. They may be isolated, partly from their deliberate withdrawal or because others have unwittingly avoided them. Also do not avoid people who are terminally ill or have lived past their life expectancy. They are in great need of personal contact. Resulting avoidance and isolation can be very painful for them.

*What to say*. The best things to say are simple and straightforward.

Examples:

- "I am sorry about your mother's death."
- "I heard of your loss and want you to know how sorry I am and I will help if I can."
- "I hurt with you."
- "I do not know what to say, but I will listen if you want to talk."
- "I am here for you."

It is *not* your responsibility to make the bereaved person feel better or to help that person through the difficult time. You should, however, make yourself available to the person, who may or may not want your help. Do not be evasive, and do not make promises you will not or can not keep. Bereaved people may be numb but they hear you and they will remember if you make empty promises. Try to think before you speak by asking yourself: "Am I saying this to make the bereaved person or myself feel better?"

Generally speaking it is better to not make any statements of "If you need anything, let me know." A person experiencing a major loss rarely has the energy to come to you. The important thing is that the reality of death is acknowledged and that you indicate your willingness to talk about it. Do *not* insist that a bereaved person talk about it. If the child does want to talk about the death, feelings, or related topics, be prepared to listen—over and over again. *Repetition* of thoughts and feelings is a large part of the healing process.

When talking about your beliefs pertaining to death, emphasize that they are *only* your beliefs; that each person has his own beliefs. Do not be too complicated in your discussion. Adapt your responses to the cognitive skills of the person or child. Do not be afraid if your discussion causes tears. It is better to cry with a person than to say, "There, there, do not cry." Crying can be a healthy and wonderful release.

In an attempt to make a grieving student feel better, it is not uncommon to hear "Your grandmother is probably in a better place now." *Do not* verbalize judgments or comparisons such as this. One life cannot be evaluated in terms of another life or how long a person lives. One life should not be equated with another. Your belief about how much better off the deceased is by being dead may be radically different than that of the bereaved!

*Do not* use stories or fantasies. They impede the grief process and generally do not facilitate understanding.

*Do not* use euphemisms. For children, to say "we lost Grandfather" implies that Grandfather will be found. If you use the euphemism of "gong to sleep" with a young child, be prepared for that child to sleep with both eyes open! If dying or death is what is meant, then say the words. A commonly used word designed to soften the term "death" is "passed". When working with children and youth, some children may wonder where the deceased passed to. Passing in the academic world has very different connotations than in the grief world!

*Do not* say such things as:

> It will be okay.
> She is in a better place.
> Good people go to heaven.
> Time heals everything.
> He is in the big _____ in the sky.
> Don't worry about it.
> He is a person on a long journey.
> God needs more angels.
> God called your daddy/mommy.
> Good people die young.

Let children come up with their own explanations.

*Accept the feelings, fears, and concerns of the grieving children.*
Assist grieving children in the expression of their feelings.
Help them to talk about their loss, regardless of whether it is a
real or fantasized loss, an anticipated loss, or an entitlement loss.
Help them discuss their feelings of guilt and anger, if any. Help
them to keep their feelings out in the open. This is an important
part of the healing process. All persons who experience grief will
feel the need to express their loss through protest, despair, and
detachment. They will need to reconsider their old thoughts and
feelings about death.

It is not atypical or aberrant for a child, adolescent, or adult
to "wish" someone dead. Wishing someone dead because of what
a person feels does not make death happen. There may, however,
be feelings of guilt as if it were their fault that the person died. "If
only I had done more . . ." Ask them if they could have that
person back, would they promise never to make that mistake
again? Their answer is likely to be "Probably not".

Even if you have unresolved difficulties about death, you
still can be an effective listener. If you feel uncertain or afraid, do
not hide your feelings. Everyone feels some inadequacy in the
face of the death of a loved one. Your struggle, when made known,
may be a demonstration to the bereaved that you care.

*Demonstrate in word and touch how much you care.* Use
physical contact where appropriate and accepted by the griever.
When a person is faced with deep and painful feelings, especially
those which make him or her feel isolated, physical contact can
be very important. Touching, when touching is needed, can
contribute so much that it outweighs the slight possibility that it
will not be desired. You should ask, "Would you like a hug?"
Sometimes touching someone can break a huge wall of defense.
One must ask, however, if this is the right time and place for
touching to occur.

*Assessment to consider* The acceptance of the reality of the
death is critical. You can not make death go away. Encourage the
grieving child in the acceptance of the **reality** of the death. The
death happened and it is final. You need to assess and take into

account the griever's strengths. Decide how much to discuss death. Respond to the signals. How does the grieving child accept the pain, sorrow, and loneliness? The acceptance of the loss has no set time or manner. Always keep in mind that children can accept the reality of their losses only as much as they are cognitively able. Do not project your way of accepting loss onto another person.

Even terminally ill patients can accept the reality of their impending deaths but they will do so at their own pace. Some can accept it easily while others deny, pace, or fight accepting their death to the very end. Again, each person has his or her own time table and way of reacting to loss.

Time may be all that you can give to a terminally ill or a grieving person. Yet giving your time may be exhausting. You may become truly weary and physically worn down by the pain, helplessness, and feelings of aloneness you feel. Pace yourself. Care for yourself. Remember to heed the message of the acronym of **HALT**: Do not let yourself get: **h**ungry, **a**ngry, **l**onely, or **t**ired.

***Death can be a growth experience.***

Experiencing the reality of death is an intensely moving experience. However, you should focus on life, not death. Encourage grieving persons to carry on with their day-to-day activities. This may help them to avoid spiraling into a deep depression. The griever needs positive, successful experiences. Losses can generate energy and the urge to keep moving, almost as if running. But grievers may do so without moving in any real direction. If this energy is turned inward, it can be very frightening and potentially destructive to the bereaved.

Because most grievers want to have some continuing bonds with the deceased, be it through memories, memorials, projects, or other ways of keeping a memory alive, it is important to continue to reinforce in them that there can be growth and light at the end of the journey, and that they will learn to live with their devastating loss. They can and will be different as they grow in strength and stamina. One does not have much of a choice here!

Be careful about causing confusion about death with the bereaved. When care-givers can not cure or "fix" a death situation, we often do not want to think or talk about it. Perhaps we do not know what to say or how to say what we are feeling about the death. Yet the bereaved children need to talk about their losses. They need to understand what are their greatest fears. They may have questions about their own deaths or who will die next or what will happen to them if someone else dies, particularly the surviving parent. Help them talk about these fears! Listen. Reassure them with real answers, not platitudes. Do not try to explain their fears to them or "fix them." Do not make promises you can not keep!

## SUGGESTIONS FOR THE CRISIS INTERVENTION TEAM

The death of a teacher, principal or classmate can be almost as devastating as the death of a family member to both students and faculty and should be acknowledged as such. The Crisis Intervention Team (CIT), if available, should be activated to provide accurate information, support, and counseling assistance for students and faculty. For schools who do not have Crisis Intervention Teams, their composition generally consists of:

- Administrator
- Guidance counselor
- Social worker
- Nurse
- Psychologist
- Teacher(s)

The function of the team is to be proactive first and then, reactive. They respond by providing a proactive, organized structure to handle school or student crises, by offering a wide range of crisis management or resolution strategies, and by working with students and staff during crisis periods. The team plans appropriate response strategies, provides services thorough counseling, assembly, class activity or staff and student support; and evaluates the effectiveness of crisis responses. The debriefing of a crisis is essential to providing best practices to students and staff members. The de-briefing and subsequent planning can be the response or reactive purpose of the team.

The involvement of the CIT is time-limited, for the period of the crisis. Because chaos and confusion are major elements surrounding death, especially untimely deaths, the CIT needs to be prepared to bring a semblance of order to the chaotic, often disorganized environment. Pre-tragedy or crisis planning is essential.

## CRISIS PLANNING TASKS

1. Comprehensive procedures should clearly define actions, roles and responsibilities of team members.
2. School faculty should receive training on how to respond to their classes when a sudden death occurs. This includes what to say to the students and what to expect in their reactions, which may vary from total hysteria to virtual disinterest.
3. Plan appropriate linkages with community resources, including the media, as needed. It is best to have **one** school spokesperson designated to communicate with the media and other outside agencies.
4. Prepare for administrative dissemination a letter that informs parents about what has happened including accurate information on the death, what the school has organized and implemented with the students on that first day,(such as offering support by allowing students to meet in groups with the CIT or appropriate Student Assistance Team members), what crisis services will be available to the students for the next few days, and what grief behaviors the parents might see in their children at home. The school should offer to make school resources available should a parent feel concern for a child.

5.  Plan to structure the days following the death with increasing focus at returning to normal. Continue to offer services for students who need to talk. An increasing return to normal schedules and classes will help to eliminate students leaving class unnecessarily. Continue to monitor student behaviors for signs of complications.

6.  If there is going to be a wake, funeral, or other service which students might attend, a Crisis Team member(s) should also attend. At a wake, funeral, or other memorial service, the Crisis Team person(s) should observe the students and offer to process their experience and feelings in a side room, if available. For many youths this may be the first time they have seen a dead body or been exposed to the death and grieving process. Sometimes a parent will offer to have students back to a safe place or home, where there is full adult supervision and support, to give the youth a time and place to share their grief and to process their feelings.

7.  About three to four weeks following the death, the CIT might begin to think of memorials with which the students have input and with which they can be actively involved. A memorial plan will help focus on life continuing and on ways to carry on the memory of the deceased.

8.  The CIT should not forget to observe faculty grieving. Offer faculty support and opportunities to remember and to memorialize too. Faculty and staff frequently give so totally to the students that they have little left to care for themselves or their grieving colleagues. Faculty need their opportunities to express their grief.

    *"GIVE SORROW WORDS . . ."* Remember that a significant death in a school system can trigger past losses that both students and staff have experienced. Do not expect everyone to mourn for the deceased. As the CIT runs groups for students and staff following school tragedies, it will become evident that many students and staff will be struggling with previous losses in their lives. Allow their

expression of all losses. Ask the students and staff directly what other deaths they have experienced. One may be surprised at the amount of death that has touched their lives.

# SENSITIVE QUESTIONS AND ANSWERS

**What should we do with the desk of a deceased student or teacher?**

Do *not* remove it! Leaving it for several days permits the reality of the loss to be acknowledged, a major task in the grieving process. When the desk and all personal belongings are immediately removed, it is perceived as an attempt to make believe the person never existed, an attempt to avoid the pain of the reality of the loss.

Students may want to periodically leave items such as notes, poems or flowers on the desk as memorials. This will allow them to accept the death and their loss naturally and give them time to get used to the desk being empty.

Students may want to discuss how the desk reminds them of the deceased. An example of this is one elementary classroom whose pet guinea pig "Digger" died. The empty cage was left in the room until the students had time to process Digger's death, their loss, and what they wanted to do with the cage. A few weeks later they decided to remove the cage and replace it with a doll house. Excellent grief resolution work by teacher and students!

**What really happened to the deceased? Why did he or she die?**
**Who will be next?**

Students and faculty need to have accurate information to dispel rumors and fears. Speak with the family of the deceased and with their permission, share whatever accurate information as is developmentally appropriate. You might ask the family of the deceased if they object to students attending the services or if they have special projects to which efforts to help could be directed.

Questions should be handled in small student groups. When a group gets as large as twenty, it is difficult to hear each child speak and to assess who is attending out of need and who is there to avoid a class. Allow the students to question and express feelings. Be aware that there will always be some inappropriate responses, such as "I am glad the guy is dead." Comments like these will often upset other students. Allow them to verbalize, normalize the responses and sort out reasons for these comments and options for responding. Remember many times there are no responses to these questions asked above. Students need to be able to ask them and come to responses that may be inconclusive.

Watch for guilt and unresolved anger issues between a student and the deceased person. When a physical education teacher died suddenly at a school, one student was concerned because he had been mad at the teacher for giving "a bad call" when officiating a sports game. He was upset that the teacher had died knowing he, the student, was angry with him for the officiating call. The boy spent nearly an hour sorting out his feelings in the group. Finally, he turned and said, "I do not think I would have done anything differently had the teacher lived." This was a process of acceptance for this young man, encouraged and facilitated by well-trained and caring staff. He had to come to this conclusion by his own reasoning process.

**How can students be helped to express their grief?**

Students will vary in their ways of expressing grief. Some students will be too numb to reminisce because of their preoccupation with the death. Some may focus on their own personal loss with seemingly mundane comments such as, "What will happen to the school dance now?" These comments are genuine expressions of loss, its impact, and they need to be acknowledged. Expression of feelings need to be received in an affirming manner. Journal writing or drawing pictures can be helpful exercises to assist students in the expression their feelings, fears or memories.

When students express feelings, they are often fearful that they are the *only* ones who feel this way. Normalize and affirm their feelings! Students grieve intermittently and may not be able to focus on grieving for extended periods of time. Allow a recess or break after discussion of the above. Try to resume some of the regular classroom schedule slowly. Remember, some of the students and staff will deal with their feelings by wanting to get back to a normal academic schedule. Also, some people will be less affected by the death than others. We should recognize the varying impacts of a death and the varying needs of the school population, including the need to resume normal schedules.

**What should the staff say about attending a funeral or other memorial service for the deceased?**

Discuss with attending students what will occur if they attend a funeral or other memorial service. Be sure to keep the discussion developmentally appropriate, succinct, and relevant! If the school staff member is uncomfortable doing this, perhaps a grief specialist could help. Be sure to keep this educationally focused. Death and funerals, wakes and memorial services can be frightening to students, so this question is touchy.

**What contact should there be with parents?**

Please be sure that students have parental approval for attending services for the deceased. Parents should take the time to explain their views and beliefs about death and memorial service occurrences with their children too. It is not just schools who educate children.

Another option would be to hold a parent meeting where the CIT member might explain all of the above and then help the parents plan how to discuss the death and the memorial process with the students. Parents are a most important link in this chain of support, and they may need school assistance on how they explain the bereavement process, on how to identify signs of

complicated grief in their children, and on how to be supportive
to their children. Continuity of support between school and home
is essential.

### What about a school memorial to the deceased student or staff member?

Memorials are beautiful ways of keeping the memory of the
deceased person alive. They are meaningful to the family of the
deceased, and they are a means of "doing something" for grieving
friends and colleagues.

Memorials come in all different sizes, plans, thoughts and
actions. Donations to a favorite charity, flowers, scholarships
are excellent, but they do not get the classmates *actively*
involved. Students can write memorials in poetry, essay or
brief paragraphs. Artistic expression in painting, drawing,
photographic collages, etc., are activities in which students
can actively participate.

Money for a scholarship or charity might be raised by students
in a student-sponsored event like a play, sports event, band concert,
fashion show, car wash, etc.

Plants, started from seeds in cups, make wonderful memorials
for younger children. Later they can be planted in a special spot
as a memorial to someone. A tree that the students raise the
money for and help plant is another way they can express their
caring. Trees and plants are highly symbolic of life and growth, a
concept that is important to continue even after someone special
dies.

### What are the trouble signs of complicated grief in students?

Look for signs of *behavior changes*, such as increased
aggression, withdrawal, increased risk taking, regression or
clumsiness that might indicate complicated grief.

After the death of a classmate, one student began to fall down
more frequently. He later explained that he fell to hide his crying

because he was sure he was the only one still sad about the death of his classmate. Children are so creative when it comes to protecting themselves from vulnerability.

# CHAPTER 10

## GUIDELINES FOR ELEMENTARY SCHOOL STAFF

Elementary age children often feel very anxious upon learning of the death of a classmate, a parent or a sibling because they themselves are so dependent upon their own parents and siblings. Loss surfaces their own fears and worries about what would happen to them if their own parent or sibling died. Further, this may be the first time they become aware of their own vulnerability to death. "Old people are supposed to die, not children or parents of young children." Some elementary school age children become fearful, overly cautious, clumsy, aggressive, regressive, withdrawn, sad or apprehensive in response to loss.

The following suggestions may be useful for elementary school teachers when working with grieving elementary school children:

* *To "give sorrow words" in a classroom situation might include* discussions as in the sharing of thoughts and feelings, drawing pictures of their feelings or memories, reading books such as *The Fall of Freddie The Leaf*, writing stories or letters to the deceased person or to the family of the deceased, or planting the seeds of a tree or flower to be planted later in a school garden in remembrance of the lost child or person. Remember that it is a myth that young children are too young to talk about their thoughts and

feelings regarding loss. In Connecticut there are wonderful grief groups for children of all ages called The Cove. The Cove operates in numerous towns and offers children structured opportunities for expressing their grief. The Cove is an incredible resource for schools in the state of Connecticut. Check in your geographical location to see what services for grieving children are available.

* *Tell the truth in terms that are chronologically, cognitively and developmentally appropriate to the student.* Provide accurate, relevant information without using euphemisms that confuse the students. Remember it is the parent's task to explain the loss. Teachers are often asked specific questions by the grieving child and may feel fearful of making inappropriate responses. It is then that this axiom applies. Do not use euphemisms such as "lost" for death. When one says "We lost Grandpa" the child may believe we will still find Grandpa if we look for him. Another euphemism is to say "We put the cat to sleep . . ." The child might be afraid to close his or her eyes! The goal is to allow the child to analyze the events and to draw personally relevant conclusions to the best of the child's developmental level. It is especially inappropriate to project our adult loss rationalizations on to our students. That is the task of the parents.

* *Avoid giving unnecessary information that serves to confuse or upset child.* In giving accurate information to students, avoid creating vivid mental images of distressing or frightening sights. Remember that young children are often left out of explanations yet they often overhear adult conversations and become frightened by what they hear. You can always contact the parents and ask them what information they would like you to give to the child.

* Elementary-age children think concretely, so *explain to them as accurately as possible what happened.* Hearing the truth may help stop wild imaginations and rumors. Out of anxiety, children may need to talk about the loss, and if

they does not have accurate information, the truth may become distorted. Let the children ask questions, and no question is silly. The children may be trying to understand the loss and the implications therein. Young children often relate the death to themselves and may seem very self absorbed. That is typical, as most children this age are very self-focused and will try to make sense of the loss as to how it impacts them.

* *Allow time for the children to share their feelings about the death.* Using "sad," "glad," "mad" as triggers for feeling words, allow them to reflect on what they (the class) feel now. Drawing pictures to express feelings or writing stories or letters that express feelings may help a child identify and understand his or her feelings safely. As stated, discussion should involve "giving sorrow words" which allows the *process* of grieving to occur.

* *All expressions by students should be affirmed, accepted, and normalized.* Honest responses, crying, sadness, or being quiet are all acceptable responses. If there is concern about a child's response, discuss concerns with appropriate school staff and if needed, a parent. (Grieving parents are often temporarily emotionally unavailable to surviving children and may need an objective assessment from the teacher as to how the grieving child is adjusting to the loss situation. Parents of children whose classmate has suffered a loss may be uninformed and thus oblivious to why their child appears upset.) Set aside time for classmate written expressions to a grieving student. Notes or pictures from school friends and teachers can be meaningful to the grieving child and family. Personal visits by the teacher, principal, and superintendent are thoughtful to the grieving family members.

* *Discussions with the class, led by the classroom teacher, might include how the children will react to a grieving student's reentry to school.* Questions to the children might center on how does the class think the student will feel upon

returning to school following the loss, how the class can welcome the child back, and what to say to the returning child. Reentry is a process, too! Many adults do not know what to say to grieving people and they often seem to say the most peculiar things!

* *Plan for the return of the bereaved student.* Students and staff frequently are uncomfortable when seeing a bereaved child returning to school and they do not know what to say to them. Guide the class and other staff members in deciding what to say and how to act when the bereaved child returns to school. Do not ignore the subject, yet be sensitive as to whether the grieving child will want to talk about the death. It is essential that the child *not* feel abandoned by friends at school during this difficult time. Grieving children already feel different due to the loss. Feeling abandoned by peers is another psychological loss! At the same time, some students will not want to discuss the loss due to their need for privacy. Educators must be respectful of the mode of grieving that is individual to each grieving student. Classmates might acknowledge the student's return from the death of a parent or sibling by saying, "I'm glad you're back, and I'm sorry your mother (brother, sister, dad) died." They should then try to resume acting as they did before the child absented for the loss.

* *Watch for changes in behavior when the grieving student returns to school.* Some elementary children develop fears of "Will I die too?" or "Will someone else I love die?" and may feel they need to remain at home to guard against further tragedy. This is their attempt to control their environment, and staying at home from school should be discouraged. Reassure the child that he or she does not have to stay at home to protect his surviving parent or sibling. If the student verbalizes fears of who will die next, assure him that most people live to be very old. Do not make promises that cannot be kept.

\* *Be aware that some elementary age children regress to a time of life when they felt more safe and secure.* They may suck their thumb or wet their pants. The life of a student who experiences death in the family has been turned upside down! Academically, elementary teachers should expect and accept a regression in the quality of work of a grieving student. Perhaps a graduated curriculum would be helpful. Be patient.

\* *Be aware that grieving students of any age are easily distracted, frequently confused and forgetful.* Emotional outbursts of anger and sadness are common. Stomach aches, headaches, eating and sleeping changes may increase as grief impacts their physical being as well as their emotional balance. Continue to focus on their positive aspects, offering love, consistency, acceptance, support, and hope.

\* Discipline is an important constant during the grief process. It should *not* be relaxed or enhanced during bereavement. *Inappropriate behavior by grieving students should not be accepted.* However, teachers need to be gentle in the redirection of the negative behavior. Students may not realize that they are angry or acting out because of feelings related to the loss of a loved one.

\* *Recognize that bereaved students may need to move around, to tell and retell the story of what happened to them, to form their own developmentally realistic understanding of the loss.* Excessive movement may be distracting behavior in the classroom but necessary to dispel the feelings of anxiety related to loss. The retelling of the story of the loss is part of the process in the development of a realistic understanding of the loss. If these behaviors impact the academics, do not lower expectations, adjust them. The child must maintain some measure of routine and school is an excellent place for that. Student self-esteem must not be damaged because of lowered concentration levels as a result of loss.

# CHAPTER 11

## GUIDELINES
## FOR MIDDLE SCHOOL
## AND HIGH SCHOOL STAFF

This age group finds great solace in one another and frequently appears to reject adult intervention. Middle school aged youth may react as described in the elementary school section or they may react more on a high school age level. Remember, a major task of adolescence is to separate from one's family of origin, and these differentiation issues and confusions consistently surface in the area of grief. Grief is the ultimate separation of attachment and often very difficult to rationalize for this age student.

Older students may not be as open with their feelings as elementary aged students. They may feel embarrassed expressing their feelings and thus bottle them up. They may feel no one understands what they have been through, which reinforces their silence.

### THE DEATH OF A PARENT, SIBLING, OR CLOSE FRIEND

Following the death of a parent, sibling, or close friend, a teacher or significant other person who is close to the grieving student might tell the child privately that he or she would like to talk with him or her. Do not say, "If you ever need to talk, let me know." Try: "I know that your mother died, and this must be very difficult for you. While we do not have to discuss your mother's death, I think it is important that we talk to be sure you are okay. At that time we can discuss whatever you would like to discuss. I'd like to see you on . . . ."

When adolescents are reluctant to speak about their feelings, ask how the student's parent, sibling, relations, or friends are handling the loss. Speaking about others can open the door of communication. It is often easier for the student to speak about other people's reactions and this strategy can smooth the way for the child to speak of his or her own reactions and emotions.

Most adolescents do not speak of their grief at home because they fear upsetting others. Death upsets family functioning and adolescents detest that. Although they often contribute to challenging the stability of a family system, that process is totally different from facing the family stressors faced in death. Youth who have suffered parental death often believe that they now have to be strong and take care of their surviving parent or siblings. This is, of course, a myth. Parents in grief need to continue parenting.

It is also common that siblings will respond differently both verbally and emotionally to loss. There often is one sibling who may be more openly demonstrative with his or her expression of grief. This expression may irritate another sibling as the manner of expression is so different from his or her's. And sometimes the expression may be actually inappropriate. Listen to whatever adolescents say about sibling expression of loss. Do not judge. Offer ways for each sibling to understand that there is no one "correct way" of expressing grief.

Think of the family system as a balanced mobile. When you remove one piece of that mobile through death, the balance is off. Children frequently respond by trying to take on the roles and responsibilities of the deceased in order to balance the system. Often these are inappropriate roles and responsibilities for adolescents to undertake, causing confusion, anger and resentment. Therefore, adult support at school can help a child sort out these feelings, fears and inappropriate roles.

# THE DEATH OF A CLASSMATE
# OR STAFF MEMBER

When this occurs, it must be openly discussed at school. The Crisis Intervention Team procedures apply once again. Much of what has been written previously for the elementary school segment is applicable here.

Adolescents treasure photographs and other memorabilia. These symbolic representations of their friends, events, and treasured moments are very powerful with teenagers. These may be vehicles which will facilitate interaction with the bereaved students. In one school a family had suffered the devastating effects of a fire that destroyed their home and all belongings. The students created a scrap book of photographs and copies of memorabilia for the children who had lost all their own picture memories in the fire.

Written expression of their feelings is often meaningful for grieving teenagers. Eulogies and memorials for the yearbook are heartfelt tributes to the deceased that help the grieving students work the healing process. Sadness, tears, expression of their feelings ("Give Sorrow Words") offer adolescents the opportunity to affirm the cleansing and healing nature of grief.

Teenagers can benefit from attending wakes, memorials, or funeral services, as they provide a sense of closure to the bereaved. As noted earlier, it may be wise to have a Crisis Intervention Team member there to assist the students in processing what they are seeing and feeling. When a teenager dies, many other teens usually attend the services, and they frequently find great solace and the beginnings of closure in these rituals. It is important to remember that they may need help in the processing of the experience.

When a teacher dies, prepare the substitute teacher for a variety of potential adolescent reactions. The substitute teacher will be feeling awkward and anxious at being asked to take the place of someone who has just died. Affirm these feelings, and share some options for dealing with potential problem areas in the classroom.

Some student reactions might be anger, resentment, feeling overwhelmed, or being weepy, stunned, and numb. The substitute teacher may be feeling similarly! Talk about it!

Continue to monitor student behavior for signs of concern with special attention to the possibility of teen suicide following the death of a family member or close friend.

## GUIDELINES FOR TALKING TO STUDENTS ABOUT DEATH

- Prepare them honestly about the serious and tragic nature of what you are about to tell them.
- Give accurate factual information regarding the death. Reassure the students that you and other staff are available and prepared to help them through this difficult time.

  Affirm and validate their reactions. Watch for body language that may signal a reaction of concern to what you told them. In students who have previously experienced death, they may react with stiffness, tension, seeming unfeeling barriers such as unconcern, or tremendous emotion. Your information regarding this death may trigger past losses and past defense mechanisms used to numb their pain when they experienced loss. Remember loss is cumulative and one loss often triggers others whether the griever realizes it or not.

  Denial and disbelief are normal reactions. Questions often are asked again and again, in more detail, in an attempt for the grieving person to grasp the impact of the death. Adolescents then typically relive when they last saw the deceased. These behaviors are attempts to accept the reality of the loss. There will be different reactions, some of which may seem hurtful or inappropriate. Respect these differences and affirm the feelings. Watch for behaviors of concern.

  Monitor for guilt and regrets. Allow for verbalization of situations that might cause a teenager to feel guilty. If the grieving student had angry words as a last interchange with the deceased, feelings of fear, guilt, anger, or worry might surface. If unchecked, these feelings can translate into aberrant behaviors.

Allow students to console one another. Observe for significant changes in behavior and/or attitude! Students typically turn to one another for solace but it is not always in the best interests of the griever. Students are children and they typically do not know how to respond other than empathically. In the event of a suicide, monitor for copy cat reactions.

Resume normal activities as appropriate. Again, remember the intensity of the grief will correlate to the degree of closeness in the relationship with the deceased; thus, there will be many students/staff who are unaffected, and they will be eager to resume normal routines. All students should be allowed to return to normal when indicated, as there is great solace and relief in returning to normal routines. Routine decreases the feelings of chaos that reign during the grief process.

Appropriate memorial planning can be very healing. It is also a key way of bringing together the students most impacted by the death and observing them for trouble signs in a covert manner.

## PARENT INVOLVEMENT

Parents are frequently uncomfortable and inexperienced in dealing with their own grief or that of their child. (As a parent and a grief professional, one of my most painful and impactful experiences was watching my son travel the journey of grief when one of his good friends was killed. I was totally unprepared for the next two years of his pain—and I was powerless to "fix it" for him. All I could do was stand silently beside him and try to maintain consistency in his totally altered world. I was also unprepared for the impact this experience had on our entire family.

We were all thrown off balance as we tried to deal with our son and brother and our own feelings of anger, loss, fear, confusion, and total powerlessness.) While grief is difficult to share, all family members are impacted by one person's journey of grief. Please be aware of this impact as school personnel deal with siblings of grieving youth.

Parent involvement is important. A letter from the principal can be written to all parents giving factual information as well as telling what services were offered at school to the students during the first days following the death. Include what professional services are available at school for the next few days, and explain to parents what grief behaviors they might see and what behaviors are normal and what are behaviors of concern. If parents are concerned about their child's grief reactions, direct them to call the school's trained Crisis Team members or other appropriate resources. This necessitates having a list of grief resources for crisis situations.

In some instances an evening meeting might be held for parents, staff, and students. The goal of the meeting, led by a certified grief therapist, is to explain the grief process, to allow ventilation of feelings, to answer questions, to offer resources, to assess how the community is dealing with the loss. It is *not* group therapy, it is educational and used to explain the healing process of grief.

Grief is not a shared experience in that no two people experience the exact same feelings, reactions, justifications, rationalizations, or modes of grief expression. This tends to make the grieving person feel totally isolated. Parents need to recognize this feeling of isolation in their grieving youngster and affirm his or her feelings to reduce this feeling of isolation. Parents need not have all the answers—in many deaths there are *NO* answers. Inherent in the grief process is the acceptance of the reality of the loss without knowing "why." Thus, when parents or friends try to explain the inexplicable, it is counterproductive. A more realistic approach is to say, "There are no answers that I can give you. But

I can listen to your questions and search with you in our attempt to make sense of this death or loss."

Parents need to know about the experiences of the grief process, the behaviors of concern and the length of the process. They need to know what resources are available when they do recognize behaviors of concern.

These resources should include community as well as school assistance options.

# CHAPTER 12

## GRIEF AND GROWTH

Grief is an ongoing process of learning to live with the loss. It is a time of life that needs the support of family, friends, and school personnel. It is a time of confusion for the student who is grieving as well as for those who are trying to be of assistance. Children and youth do not suffer loss easily yet with the proper assistance, they can not only learn to live with their losses, but grow and actually learn from the experiences. Loss is a part of life. Since we are all experts at developmental losses, we as educators and teachers must teach children how to learn from these events and thus, be able to transfer that learning to the more catastrophic loss situations that they will face.

Remember, that loss can have several meanings to children and youth. Loss can be that of a parent, sibling, pet, or other important relationship. The loss can be due to death, divorce, relocation, addiction, mental illness, chronic illness, to name but a few. The nature of the relationship with the loss is the essential factor in the resolution of grief.

Loss can be the fear of losing something highly valued such as an award or title. Students who are involved in intense dating relationships are often terrified of their partner finding someone else, which obviously often occurs and thus is a valid fear.

And it is possible for students to anticipate something such as a college acceptance, not get it, and feel a tremendous sense of loss.

Children of different ages and maturity levels have grief responses that are directly related to their developmental maturity level. Do not expect all children to respond to loss situations in the same way or to have the same needs. The grief response process is unique and individual to the griever. There are some commonalities in the treatment of children in grief. The most basic strategies are to listen, observe, and be present with the child.

A final word of caution to all care givers working with children in grief: remember that students who have suffered losses need to be monitored for months following their losses. Symptoms of their grief may not surface until one to three years later. And theses symptoms may manifest themselves in ways that seem unrelated to the losses. Thus, be alert for changes in behavior for several years following the loss.

Grief as a growth process continues, even for this author. It is a lifelong process.

# REFERENCES

Doka, Kenneth. *Disenfranchised Grief.*New York: Lexington Books, 1989.

Edelman, Hope. *Motherless Daughters: The Legacy of Loss*. New York: Addison—Wesley, 1994.

Ginsburg, Genevieve. *Widow to Widow. Tucson, AZ:* Fisher Books 1997.

Gordon, Audrey, and Klass, Dennis. *They Need to Know, How to Teach Children About Death*. Englewood Cliffs, NJ: Prentice-Hall, 1979.

Grollman, Earl A., Ed. *Explaining Death to Children*. Boston: Beacon Press, 1969.

Grollman, Earl A., Ed. *Talking About Death: A Dialogue Between Parent, Child*. Boston: Beacon Press, 1976.

Harris, Maxine. *The Loss that is Forever: The Lifelong Impact of the Early Death of a Mother or Father*. New York: Dutton, 1996.

Jewett, Claudia L. *Helping Children Cope with Separation and Loss*. Harvard, MA: The Harvard Common Press, 1982.

Kubler-Ross, Elisabeth. *On Death and Dying*. New York: MacMillan Publishing, 1969.

Kubler-Ross, Elisabeth. *Questions and Answers on Death and Dying*. New York: MacMillan Publishing, 1974.

Kushner, Harold S. *When Bad Things Happen to Good People*. New York: Avon Books, 1981.

Lord, Janice Harris. *Beyond Sympathy: How to Help Another Through Injury, Illness or Loss*. Ventura, CA: Pathfinder, 1994.

Lord, Janice Harris. *No Time for Goodbyes, Lord: Coping with Sorrow, Anger, and Injustice After a Tragic Death*. Ventura, CA: Pathfinder, 1994.

Rando, Therese: *Treatment of Complicated Mourning*, Champaign, Il. Research Press, 1993.

Rando, Therese. *Grief, Dying, and Death*. Champaign, Il. Research Press, 1984.

Schaeffer, Dan, and Christine Lyons. *How Do We Tell the Children*. New York: Newmarket Press, 1993.

Walsh, Froma, and Monica McGoldrick. *Living Beyond Loss: Death in the Family*. New York: W.W. Norton, 1991.

# RECOMMENDED RESOURCES

## BOOKS FOR ADULTS

Buscaglia, L. *The Fall of Freddie the Leaf.* New York: St. Martins Press, 1982.

Cohn, Janice. *I Had a Friend Named Peter.* New York: Morrow and Company, 1987.

Edelman, Hope. *Motherless Daughters: The Legacy of Loss.* New York: Addison—Wesley, 1994.

Galinsky, N. *When a Grandchild Dies: What to Do, What to Say, How to Cope.* Houston, TX: Gal in Sky Publishing Company, 1999.

Gerner, M.H. *For Bereaved Grandparents.* Omaha, NE, Centering Corporation, 1990.

Ginsburg, Genevieve. *Widow to Widow. Tucson, AZ:* Fisher Books 1997.

Gordon, Audrey, and Klass, Dennis. *They Need to Know, How to Teach Children About Death.* Englewood Cliffs, NJ: Prentice-Hall, 1979.

Grollman, Earl A., Ed. *Explaining Death to Children.* Boston: Beacon Press, 1969.

Grollman, Earl A., Ed. *Talking About Death: A Dialogue Between Parent, Child.* Boston: Beacon Press, 1976.

Harris, Maxine. *The Loss that is Forever: The Lifelong Impact of the Early Death of a Mother or Father.* New York: Dutton, 1996.

Jewett, Claudia L. *Helping Children Cope with Separation and Loss.* Harvard, MA: The Harvard Common Press, 1982.

Kubler-Ross, Elisabeth. *Questions and Answers on Death and Dying*. New York: MacMillan Publishing, 1974.

Kushner, Harold S. *When Bad Things Happen to Good People*. New York: Avon Books, 1981.

Lord, Janice Harris. *Beyond Sympathy: How to Help Another Through Injury, Illness or Loss*. Ventura, CA: Pathfinder, 1994.

Lord, Janice Harris. *No Time for Goodbyes, Lord: Coping with Sorrow, Anger, and Injustice After a Tragic Death*. Ventura, CA: Pathfinder, 1994.

Reed, M. L. *Grandparents Cry Twice*. Amityville, NY, Baywood, 2000.

Schaeffer, Dan, and Christine Lyons. *How Do We Tell the Children*. New York: Newmarket Press, 1993.

Schweibert, P. *A Grandparent's Sorrow*, Portland, OR: Perinatal Loss, 1996.

Walsh, Froma, and Monica McGoldrick. *Living Beyond Loss: Death in the Family*. New York:
W.W. Norton, 1991.

# BOOKS FOR CHILDREN

**For Children Ages Three to Five**

Brown, Margaret Wise. *The Dead Bird*. New York: Young Scott Books, 1958.

Carrick, Carol. *The Accident*. New York: Seabury Press, 1976.

DePaola, Tomie. *Nana Upstairs and Nana Downstairs*. New York: G. P. Putnam's Sons, 1973.

Johnson, Joy and Marv. *Where's Jess?* NE: Centering Corporation, 1982, Revision 1992.

Palmer, Pat. *I Wish I Could Hold Your Hand*. New York: Impact Publishers, 1994.

Peavy, Linda. *Allison's Grandfather*. New York: Charles Scribners Sons, 1981.

Rothman, Juliet. *A Birthday Present for Daniel*. New York: Continuum, 1995.

Sanford, Doris. *It Must Hurt A Lot*. Portland, OR: Multnomah Press, 1985.

Simon, Norma. *We Remember Philip*. Niles, IL: A. Whitman, 1979.

Stein, Sara Bonnett. *About Dying: An Open Family Book for Parents and Children Together*. New York: Walker & Company, 1974.

Zolotow, Charlotte. *If You Listen*. New York: Harper and Row, 1980.

Zolotow, Charlotte. *My Grandson Lew*. New York: Harper and Row, 1974.

**For Children Ages Five to Eight**

Bartoli, Jennifer. *Nonna*. New York: Harvey House, 1975.

Bernstein, Joanne. *When People Die*. New York: Irwin and Company, 1977.

Brown, Laurie K. and Marc Brown. *When Dinosaurs Die*. Boston: Little. Brown, 1996.

Clifton, Lucille. *Everett Anderson's Goodbye*. New York, Holt and Co. 1983.

Cohen, Miriam. *Jim's Dog Muffins*. New York: Greenwillow Books, 1984.

Coutant, Helen. *The First Snow*. New York: Knopf, 1974.

Fassler, Joan. *My Grandpa Died Today*. New York: Human Science Press, Inc., 1983.

Holden, L. Dwight. *Gran-Gran's Best Trick*. New York: Magination Press, 1989

Mellonie, Bryan, and Robert Ingpen. *Lifetimes*. New York: Bantam Doubleday Dell, 1987.

Mills, Joyce. *Gentle Willow*. Milwaukee, WI.: Gareth Stevens Publishing, 1994.

O'Toole, Donna. *Aarvy Aardvark Finds Hope*.—: Rainbow Connection, 1997.

Scrivani, Mark. *Love, Mark: A Journey Through Grief*. Syracuse, NY: Hope For Bereaved, Inc., 1990.

Scrivani, Mark. *Love, Mark: Companions on the Journey*. Syracuse, NY: Hope For Bereaved, Inc., n.d.

Sims, Alvin. *Am I Still a Sister?* Albuquerque, NM: Big A & Company, 1986.

Smith, Doris Buchanon. *A Taste of Blackberries*. New York: Crowell, 1976.

Thomas, Pat. *I Miss You*. New York: Barrons. 2001.

Van den Berg, Marinus. *The Three Birds,* 1994.

Viorst, Judith. *The Tenth Good Thing About Barney*. New York: Atheneum, 1971.

## For Children Ages Eight to Twelve

Blue, Rose. *Grandma Didn't Wave Back*. New York: Franklin Watts, 1972.

Bradbury, Bianca. *I've Vinny. I'm Me*. Boston: Houghton Mifflin, 1977.

Byars, Betsy. *Goodbye Chicken Little*. New York: Harper, 1979.

Carter, Forest. *The Education of Little Tree*. New Mexico, University of New Mexico Press, 1976.

Clardy, Andrea F. *Dusty Was My Friend*. New York: Humane Science Press, 1984.

Cleaver, Vera and Bill. *Grover*. Philadelphia: Lippincott, 1970.

Farley, Carol. *The Garden is Doing Fine*. New York: Bantam Books, 1983.

Greene, Constance C. *Beat the Turtle Drum*. New York: Viking, 1976.

Hanson, Warren. *The Next Place*. Minneapolis: Waldman House Press, 1997.

Heegaard, Marge. *When Someone Very Special Dies*. Minneapolis: Woodland Press, 1991.

LaShan, Eda. *Learning to Say Goodbye: When a Parent Dies*. New York: MacMillan, 1976.

Levine, Jennifer. *Forever in My Heart*. Surnsville, NC: Mountain Rainbow Publications, 1992.

Levy, Erin Linn. *Children are not Paper Dolls*. Incline Village, NV: The Publisher's Mark, 1982.

Mann, Peggy. *There are Two Kinds of Terrible*. New York: Doubleday, 1977.

McLendon, Gloria. *My Brother Joey Died*. New York: Julian Messner, 1982.

Mellonie, Bryan, and Robert Ingren. *Lifetimes*. New York: Bantam Books, 1983.

Powell, E. Sandy. *Geranium Morning*. Minneapolis: Carolrhoda Books, Inc. 1990.

Rolfes, Eric. *The Kids Book About Death and Dying*. N.p., 1985.

Thomas, Jane Resh. *Saying Good-bye to Grandma*. New York: Clarion Books, 1988.

Van den Berg, Marinus. The Three Birds: *A Story for Children About the Loss of a Loved One*. New York: Magination Press, 1994.

Wilhelm, Hans. *I'll Always Love You*. New York: Crown Publishers, Inc. 1985.

### Books for Young People Ages Twelve Years and Up

Agee, James. *A Death in the Family*. New York: Avon, 1959.

Berkus, Rusty. *To Heal Again*. Encino, CA: Red Rose Press, 1986.

Carner, Charles. *Tawny*. New York: MacMillan, 1978.

Cleaver, Vera and Bill. *Where the Lilies Bloom*. Philadelphia: Lippincott, 1969.

Coburn, John B. *Anne and the Sand Dobbies*. New York: Seabury Press, 1964.

Diamond, Donna. *Bridge To Terabithia*. New York: Avon Books, 1977.

Fahy, Mary. *The Tree that Survived the Winter*. New York: Paulist Press, 1989.

Garden, Nancy. *The Loners*. New York: Viking, 1972.

Gunther, John. *Death Be Not Proud*. New York: Harper, 1949.

Grollman, Earl A. *Straight Talk about Death for Teenagers: How to Cope with Losing Someone You Love*. MA. Beacon Press, 1993.

Kremitz, Jill. *How It Feels When a Parent Dies*. New York: Alfred Knopf, 1981.

Lewis, C. S. *A Grief Observed*. New York: Bantam Books, 1961.

Sims, Alicia M. *Am I Still a Sister?* Los Angeles; Big A & Company, 1986.

Slote, Alfred. *Hang Tough, Paul Mather*. New York: Lippincott, 1973.

Shriver, Maria. *What's Heaven?* New York: St. Martin's Press. 1999.

Woodford, Peggy. *Please Don't Go*. New York: Dutton, 1973.

## CURRICULA FOR SUPPORT GROUPS

Bebensee, Barbara, Ed.D. *Perspectives on Loss*. Arvada, CO: TLC Publications, 1985.

Beckman, Roberta. *Children Who Grieve*. Revised Edition, Florida: Learning Publications, 1999.

Family Life Office. *Growing Through Change*. Archdiocese of Omaha, Nebraska, 1990.

Haasl, Beth, and Jean Marnocha. *Bereavement Support Group Program for Children*. Philadelphia: Brunner-Routledge, 1999.

## CATALOGS AND PUBLISHERS OF GRIEF RESOURCES

*Caregiving and End of Life Resources*. Minneapolis, MN. Phone: 800 544-8207.

*Centering Corporation's Grief Resources*. Omaha, NE. Phone: 402 553-1200.

*Compassion Books*. Burnsville, NC. Phone: 800 970-4220.

*Illness/Bereavement Caregiving and Counseling Resources*. Weaverville, CA. Boulden Publishing. Phone: 800 238-8433.

*Resources for Meeting Life's Challenges*. Dubuque, IA. Islewest Publishing. Phone: 800 557-9867.

# VIDEOS

*Aquarius* Health Care Videos. Sherborn, MA. Phone: 508 651-2963.

# SOME INTERNET BOOK RESOURCES

*Cancer Patient Education Program*
*http://cancer.duke.edu/pated/books:* This site has resources for all ages, some more directly related to the terminal illness process and how to talk with children about that process, be it for them as the terminally ill or for a significant adult.

*Coquitlam Public Library*
*http://library.coquitlam.bc.ca/children/death.htm.* This site offers more educational resources for children of all ages.

*WidowNet*
*http://www.fortnet.org/WidowNet:* This site that has its own extensive grief book listing submitted by readers.